From Wend

W9-BZW-327

Praise for GOING PLACES WITH GOD

The genius of this devotional book is that it finds vital, life-changing truth in the details of the Scriptures. Wayne Stiles not only reveals what these details mean but also shows why they matter for your life. *Going Places with God* is an encouraging and unique journey through God's Word. I highly recommend it.

TODD BOLEN

BiblePlaces.com
Associate Professor of Biblical Studies
Israel Bible Extension, The Master's College

Want to have your quiet time in Israel each morning? If so, this is the book for you. In this series of short devotionals, Wayne Stiles will take you on a magnificent spiritual journey to the land of the Bible. Each day, you will have the privilege of walking through the land as you read the Word . . . and then ponder its significance for your life today.

DR. CHARLES DYER

Provost and Dean of Education, Moody Bible Institute

In this devotional book, *Going Places with God*, Wayne Stiles has captured the heart of Israel. Page after page, you will see the sights, hear the sounds and feel the pulse of this ancient land of the Bible as you retrace the steps of Jesus. Not only that, but Wayne's personal insights will help you begin each day with an attitude of prayer, centeredness and thanksgiving.

MARY GRAHAM

President, Women of Faith

Going Places with God is a thoroughly unique and refreshing approach to daily devotionals. Wayne Stiles uses his extensive knowledge of the Holy Land to usher the reader into a "You are there" devotional tour of Israel, helping us not only trod where the Bible characters trod, but also learn the lessons God had for them in their setting. Prepare to be personally challenged and spiritually invigorated!

DAVID GREGORY

Best-selling Author, *Dinner with a Perfect Stranger* and *Day with a Perfect Stranger*

Wayne Stiles has been one of the most knowledgeable, innovative and creative people I've worked with in ministry. You will find all of these attributes in this devotional. Wayne combines biblical interpretation, personal application and historical quotations to make a unique and enjoyable mix.

TOMMY NELSON
Senior Pastor, Denton Bible Church
Author, *The Book of Romance*

Looking at how God shaped the lives of His people through the places He took them offers us tremendous insight into our own spiritual journey. Wayne Stiles has given us more than an inspiring and refreshing look at the lands of the Bible . . . he has given us strength for the journey home.

JOSEPH M. STOWELL
Teaching Pastor, Harvest Bible Chapel
Former President, Moody Bible Institute

From Titus's legions torching the Holy of Holies in Jerusalem to today's Hezbollah rocket attacks, the battle still rages over who will rule the Promised Land. Wayne Stiles loves Israel. More importantly, he loves the ultimate Savior and Lord over Israel and the world. This devotional turns biblical geography into a challenge to walk intimately with our Savior. It will do more than warm your heart. It will transform your life.

DR. DAVID B. WYRTZEN
Pastor-Teacher, Midlothian Bible Church
Adjunct Professor, Dallas Theological Seminary

WAYNE STILES

GOING PLACES
WITH GOD

A DEVOTIONAL JOURNEY THROUGH
THE LANDS OF THE BIBLE

Regal

From Gospel Light
Ventura, California, U.S.A.

PUBLISHED BY REGAL BOOKS
FROM GOSPEL LIGHT
VENTURA, CALIFORNIA, U.S.A.
PRINTED IN THE U.S.A.

All Scripture quotations, unless otherwise indicated, are taken from the *New American Standard Bible,* © 1960, 1962, 1963, 1968, 1971, 1972, 1973, 1975, 1977, 1995 by The Lockman Foundation. Used by permission.

Other versions used are
CSB—Holman Christian Standard Bible. © 2001, Broadman and Holman Publishers, Lifeway Christian Resources, 127 Ninth Avenue North, Nashville, TN 37234.
NIV—Scripture taken from the *Holy Bible, New International Version®.* Copyright © 1973, 1978, 1984 by International Bible Society. Used by permission of Zondervan Publishing House. All rights reserved.
NLT—Scripture quotations marked (*NLT*) are taken from the *Holy Bible,* New Living Translation, second edition, copyright © 2004. Used by permission of Tyndale House Publishers, Inc., Wheaton, Illinois 60189. All rights reserved.

Published in association with the literary agency of Mark Sweeney & Associates, Bonita Spring, FL 34135.

Maps on pages 28-29, 42-43, 56-57, 70-71, 84-85 and 98-99 reproduced from datasets. Copyright © 2005 BibleWorks, LLC. The source of underlying data for some of the images was the Global Land Cover Facility, http://www. landcover.org. All rights reserved.
Maps on pages 112-113 reproduced from Barry J. Beitzel, *The Moody Atlas of Bible Lands* (Chicago: Moody Press, 1985), pp. 165, 203. Used by permission.
Maps on pages 126-127 reproduced from James M. Monson and H. T. Frank, *Student Map Manual, Historical Geography of the Bible Lands* (Jerusalem: Pictorial Archive Near Eastern History Est., 1979), Map 11-3.

Library of Congress Cataloging-in-Publication Data
Stiles, Wayne.
Going places with God / Wayne Stiles.
p. cm.
ISBN 0-8307-4316-2 (hard cover) — ISBN 0-8307-4356-1 (international trade paper)
1. Meditations. 2. Devotional calendars. I. Title.
BV4811.S835 2006
242'.2—dc22
       2006027412

1   2   3   4   5   6   7   8   9   10 / 10   09   08   07   06

Rights for publishing this book in other languages are contracted by Gospel Light Worldwide, the international nonprofit ministry of Gospel Light. Gospel Light Worldwide also provides publishing and technical assistance to international publishers dedicated to producing Sunday School and Vacation Bible School curricula and books in the languages of the world. For additional information, visit www.gospellightworldwide.org; write to Gospel Light Worldwide, P.O. Box 3875, Ventura, CA 93006; or send an e-mail to info@gospellightworldwide.org.

march 2008

With my love and great
thanksgiving for
our friendship in Christ,
Wendy

❖

FOR CATHY, SARAH AND KATIE

❖

IF I TOLD YOU EARTHLY THINGS

AND YOU DO NOT BELIEVE,

HOW WILL YOU BELIEVE IF I TELL

YOU HEAVENLY THINGS?

JOHN 3:12

CONTENTS

FOREWORD

I remind myself most every year of the words of Socrates: "The unexamined life is not worth living."

That statement rings true because over time things tend to get complicated. We begin our Christian life with utter delight and simplicity. But as tradition, religion, and too many activities begin to pile on top of what was originally there, the simplicity gets lost.

I thought of that several times in a recent visit to the Holy Land. Frequently people come to Israel to walk where Jesus walked. They often ask their guide, "Did Jesus walk here?" Unscrupulous guides will say, "Oh, yes, He was in *that* church and He probably saw *that* building." But honest guides pause and say, "Come here, let me show you something." And they walk over to a precipice and lean over a fence. "Look down there about 25 feet," the guide says. "Do you see those stones? Jesus *may* have walked there." Then the traveler begins to realize that over the passing of centuries and numerous wars, the sands of time have slowly covered multiple feet of the original site. Sometimes there's a twinge of disappointment, but I always look forward to those places where we can say for sure, "Jesus walked here."

For example, we know He walked on the Sea of Galilee. There's no way to build a church over that! There's no pile of rubbish, stack of debris or rocks for people to kiss. All the stuff of tradition and religious veneer is conspicuously absent—it's just water. It's the same surface Jesus walked on. There you see the same shore where He called some of His disciples to leave their nets and follow Him. It's an amazing feeling to be right there where they were. It's an eye-opening thrill to see what they saw! The old sea has become one of Cynthia's and my favorite places on the planet. Why? Because we have returned to the original. It's the simple, uncomplicated, quiet place where we renew something that has gotten buried over the years.

Has your walk with Christ become buried? Time has a way of doing that (remember, time complicates things). After a series of heartbreaking experiences, overwhelming obstacles, wrong decisions and maybe an abusive church or two, it's easy to lose your way. That's why periodically we need to reexamine our lives.

My friend and colleague Wayne Stiles has a contagious enthusiasm for the land of Israel. I know; I've traveled there with him more than once! *Going Places with God* is the result of years of study, many weeks of travel, and a sincere passion to reveal how the Bible's places affected the Bible's people . . . and how they can affect our lives today.

In a world that has lost its way and in a culture that has drifted far from truth, how helpful it is to return to the Bible's uncomplicated command, "Draw near to God and He will draw near to you" (James 4:8). Here the Scripture offers us a promise—*a motivation*—to unearth our walk with Christ. When I draw near to God, He draws near to me. *It's wonderful!*

As the next few months unfold, what better time to gain a fresh perspective on your Bible and to remove the rubble that has buried your walk with Christ? Let me encourage you, as you journey through these pages to some sacred places—allow the simplicity of each scene to rekindle your relationship with Him.

My hope is that very soon you will discover the rubble is gone and the debris is cleared away, as you find yourself walking where Jesus walked. In reality . . . you will find yourself walking intimately with Him.

Charles R. Swindoll

ACKNOWLEDGMENTS

Pascal wrote in *Pensées*, "The last thing one settles in writing a book is what one should put in first." For me, thanks ought to come first.

The shaping of a book comes from the shaping of a life, and I guess any author's first work tends to thank too many people. So, while I'm tempted to mention everyone from my newest colleague to my first guitar teacher (for whom I'm extremely grateful), I'll mention only a few individuals . . . and fail to mention many more.

Thanks to Dr. Charlie Dyer for awakening my love for biblical geography and for capably leading Cathy and me on our first tour of Israel. My goal is to go to Israel more times than you. Thanks to Dr. Dave Wyrtzen, my mentor and friend, for consistently challenging me to make the biblical, historical Jesus my Lord and not just my topic of study. Thanks to Todd Bolen for his suggestions, corrections and friendship. Thanks to Robert Billingslea for his consistent voice of encouragement.

Thanks to Mark Sweeney for believing enough in my writing to represent and encourage me. Are all agents as good as you? Thanks to Steve Lawson and his team at Regal Books for their excitement over this project from beginning to end and for striving to create settings of silver for my apples of gold.

Thanks to Mel and Tom, who instilled in me a passion for my Bible and introduced me to Dallas Theological Seminary. Thanks to the elders and congregations of Denton Community Church and Denton Bible Church, with whom I labored as best friends in the ministry for over 15 years. I miss you.

Thanks to Chuck and Cynthia for the privilege of serving with you . . . and for modeling the grace you teach (it's so refreshing to see the real thing). Thanks to the Creative Ministries department, and all the staff of Insight for Living, for your professionalism, sense of humor and friendship.

Thanks to my father for infusing in me a strong work ethic and to my mother (now in God's presence) for giving me life. Thanks to my sister, Courtney Chavanell, for loving Mom so patiently and to my brother, Matt Stephens, for renewing my faith that God can transform a life. Thanks to Walt Stephens for taking a proactive role in the life of my family and for displaying, along with Sherry, strength in the face of struggle.

Great appreciation goes to Sarah and Katie for striving to have godly character, for reading the Scriptures daily, and for being daughters any daddy would be proud of.

And, if I may borrow from Pascal's quote, I'd say, "The first thing one settles in writing acknowledgements is whom one should thank last." I'm grateful most of all to my wife, Cathy, my first and best editor, for all the pencil marks that made a better manuscript . . . and for all the conversations that have made me a better man. I'm honored to journey through life with you.

INTRODUCTION

Everything happened somewhere.

And often in our lives, the places we remember as special stay with us because of something special that happened there. Think of the places most significant to you . . . perhaps the camp where you accepted Christ; the old barn where you became engaged; the park where your firstborn learned to walk; maybe even the house where you lost a loved one. What makes these places so special? Most likely, it's not the places themselves but the events that took place there.

But in biblical times, the place itself often played a major role in the significant events that occurred there. Beside the place where water gushed from the ground, there a man drove his tent stake—and so laid the foundation of a city. Rains ran through immovable ravines, and beside those rivers people cultivated their fields and watered their livestock. Where the easiest ground to travel lay, there a wayfarer walked—and so a highway began. Geography affects history.

Trace any civilization back to its origin, and geography provides the stage for history's drama. Be it a strategic military position, an abundant water supply or a convenient traveling route, geography determined, to a great extent, where the events occurred.

This book finds its roots in places God chose—literally. The lands of the Bible offer more than a backdrop for the stories of the Bible. These places played an integral role in shaping the lives of those who lived there. God designed it so. And for us, understanding how the land shaped its inhabitants gives us tremendous insight into understanding Scripture. Even more, it provides us with a glimpse as to why God has placed us where we live today.

God takes us places we would never choose that we might become what we've always wanted to be—that is, *all that He created us to be*. God is much bigger than we can imagine. Thus, He wants for us more than we ever dreamed.

God wants us to *trust* Him, and so do we. He wants us to *glorify* Him, to *know* Him, and so do we. But really, we often want to trust God only when we understand Him. We want to glorify God in our success—not in our struggles. And our desire to know Him slices His list of attributes in half. When we settle for anything less than all of God, we settle for less than all we can become. We can't help all this. If we could, we wouldn't have needed a Savior. The Lord Jesus has a good deal more for us than salvation. Conversion to Christ provides *but the beginning* of the good work He will do in us—and the good works He has prepared for us to do.

So God takes us places. He takes us places we cannot control. He puts us in settings we don't understand, places that compel us to trust Him. In these sacred places, He reveals the weakness of our hearts so that we learn not to depend on ourselves. As our weak grip gives way, we discover the joy of our weakness is His strength—which carried us all along.

21

Biblical characters and their places offer ideal fodder for daily devotions, for they provide us with a view into how God shapes our own lives through the locations He has placed us. Just as God led Abraham to Canaan, Joseph to Egypt, and Jesus' disciples to the ends of the earth, so God takes us places to learn lessons of provision, protection, providence and persuasion. Just as God fashioned the land of Israel to develop the spiritual lives of His people, so too He shapes our circumstances for the same reason.

We discover that the God who seemed a sadist in our struggles has loved us despite our doubts and discouragement. As with Jacob by the Jabbok, God allows us first to struggle *against* Him, then to struggle *with* Him, and then, at last, to struggle *for* Him so that as we surrender, we become more like the one who prayed in Gethsemane, "Not my will, but yours be done." We become all He created us to be.

We can only grow to be like Christ as we know Christ—all of Him. So God takes us places we would never choose in order to give us what we could never receive anywhere else—Himself.

Let's begin this journey together—to these places of His choosing.

The beautiful dome of the Church of the Holy Sepulcher in Jerusalem crowns the traditional site of Jesus Christ's burial and resurrection.

A GOOD PLACE TO BEGIN

GENESIS 1–2

From the first verse of Scripture, God revealed how the earth set the stage for the divine drama of history to take place (see Gen. 1:1). From its formless, void beginning, the Lord fashioned the earth with intent in its details. From this ground, God made physical man a spiritual being in His image.

The Lord planted two trees in the Garden of Eden (see Gen. 2:8-9). Adam's physical need required him to make a spiritual choice: From which tree would he eat? Would he obey God's command not to eat from the tree of the knowledge of good and evil?

God originally inspired the book of Genesis for a people about to enter yet another land He had prepared. That land would hold the direst of geographical conditions, placing them in a situation similar to Adam's. Would they obey God's commands? "I have set before you life and death," God would tell them. "So choose life" (Deut. 30:19). Centuries later, Jesus also found Himself facing a similar temptation in this barren land—and He clung to God's Word (see Matt. 4:1-10).

Whether in Eden or Canaan or California, our decision remains the same. The land where we live—be it lush or desolate—is the stage on which we act out God's glory. Regardless of our location or influences, God gives us a choice each day from which tree to eat. In every case, life or death comes from our response to God's Word.

As you commit to spending time in the Bible, commit also to obeying what your Creator reveals each day: "For it is not an idle word for you; indeed it is your life" (Deut. 32:47).

> *My Creator, whatever place I find myself this year, my duty remains the same: to choose life by obedience to whatever You teach me in Your Word and thus display Your image wherever You take me in Your world. I devote to You this year . . . and this day. Be glorified in it, O God.*

Either the Bible will keep you away from sin, or sin will keep you away from the Bible. —*C. S. Lewis*

See maps on pages 28-29, 56-57.

WHERE HE LEADS ME

MATTHEW 2:13-23

Almost 2,000 years before Joseph and Mary journeyed to Bethlehem, Jacob and Rachel, another expectant couple, traveled the same road. Rachel gave birth to Benjamin, but she died after delivery, and Jacob buried her near Bethlehem (see Gen. 35:19). Rachel's death foreshadowed the devastation that the territory of Benjamin would suffer in Jeremiah's time: "Rachel is weeping for her children . . . because they are no more" (Jer. 31:15; see also Matt. 2:17-18).

Yet the prophecy found its final fulfillment in Jesus' day, when Herod the Great slaughtered all baby boys in Bethlehem. So, at God's direction, Joseph took Mary and Jesus to Egypt to live until Herod's death.

Each movement of Jesus' family finds its cause in God's revelation to Joseph—fleeing Bethlehem to Egypt, returning from Egypt to Israel, avoiding Judea to settle in Galilee. God's purposes for these moves lay first in the protection of His Son, but Matthew notes that each directive also fulfilled Scripture. Doubtless anyone but God saw beforehand the murky prophecies fulfilled by these geographic moves. But in hindsight, they become clear.

As we strain to see tomorrow with all its uncertainties, we can take comfort that our God sees the future as clearly as the past. He seldom gives us all we need in order to understand, but He always gives us all we need to obey. Eventually, we discover that in our simple obedience to God's Word, He has guided us along paths far too complex for us to see at the time. He leads us with His wise—but often unusual—directives, always rooted in Scripture, for our good and for His glory.

Lord, tomorrow is unknown, but You are already there. While I often don't understand Your leading, I honestly don't want to go anywhere else. As with all years past, I know that You will provide, You will guide, and I will follow.

Follow Providence as far as it agrees with the Word, and no farther.
—*John Flavel*

See maps on pages 56-57, 98-99, 126-127.

IT IS WRITTEN

MATTHEW 3:17–4:10

The devil hurled a challenge at Jesus based on the affirmation the Father had just given at Jesus' baptism: "This is My beloved Son, in whom I am well-pleased" (Matt. 3:17). So Satan's temptation followed suit: "If You are the Son of God, command that these stones become bread" (4:3). Matthew tells us that in preparation for Jesus' temptation in the wilderness, He fasted for more than a month—and He became very hungry.

Just east of this locale, across the Jordan River in the Plains of Moab, Moses had penned the Scriptures that Jesus would use in response to Satan's temptations. Jesus quoted from Deuteronomy 8, a passage of Scripture in which Moses reminded Israel how God had tested them during their 40 years in the wilderness in order to know what was in their hearts. He allowed them to hunger, and then He fed them with manna. All this He did to teach them, as Jesus quoted, "Man shall not live on bread alone, but on every word that proceeds out of the mouth of God" (v. 4).

Satan tempts at opportune times of vulnerability and need. Jesus hungered. But temptation always offers to fulfill a legitimate need in an illegitimate way. Every temptation Christ endured took place at a different location and had a different motivation, but Jesus' response remained the same: "It is written . . ." Christ's response shows us that regardless of the nature of our temptations, the Word of God holds the truth we must draw from to stand firm. When temptation squeezes, Scripture should spill out.

Help me to learn, Father, that what temptation offers it takes back exponentially, for its benefits invest only in my destruction. Give me today the focus of Jesus, who clung to truth in the face of every evil enticement.

Satan goes on with mankind as he began with them . . . by appearing to be a friend to their happy state, and pretending to advance it to higher degrees. —*Jonathan Edwards*

See maps on pages 84-85, 98-99.

A STRATEGIC MOVE

MATTHEW 4:13-25

Few went to Nazareth unless they had to go there—the city sat off the beaten path and high on a hill. Yet it was the perfect place for the boy Jesus to grow up in safe seclusion, away from the grasp of any who might seek to harm Him (see Matt. 2:21-23).

Years later, at the beginning of His ministry, Jesus moved His base of operations from the sleepy town of Nazareth to the bustling Capernaum by the Sea of Galilee. Matthew notes how this move fulfilled "what was spoken through Isaiah the prophet" (4:14). While several cities along the shore could have fulfilled this prophecy, it seems that Jesus' selection of Capernaum had more deliberate purposes.

A thriving fishing village, Capernaum straddled the international highway that stretched from Syria to Egypt. By choosing Capernaum, Jesus selected a city that enjoyed a constant flow of people who could carry His message to many places. And that's just what happened. As Jesus preached in Galilee, "news about Him spread throughout all Syria" (v. 24). Not only did travelers take the news north into Syria, but they also took it by other roads into "Galilee and the Decapolis and Jerusalem and Judea and from beyond the Jordan" (v. 25).

In our lives and ministries, we must not merely exist but also live strategically. What represents the best use of our time for God's glory? In what location or vocation can we best serve the Lord? Sometimes, these answers require a major move—as was the case with Jesus. But sometimes, we simply need to change our thinking and ask ourselves, *Is the kingdom of God really the goal of my life?*

Lord Jesus, rather than pursuing a place to hide where I can escape the irritation of people and culture's corruption, help me to see my world through Your eyes. Place me in places where I can have the greatest influence for Your kingdom. Show me today how to seek first the kingdom of God—above my own preferences.

I will place no value on anything I have or possess unless it is in relationship to the kingdom of God. —David Livingstone

See maps on pages 28-29, 56-57, 70-71, 112.

TO THE LAND I WILL SHOW YOU

GENESIS 12:1-3

Genesis began with God blessing all He created. But the fall of man, Abel's murder, the rebellion at Babel and the global flood gave cause to doubt that there would be any recovery of that blessing. Genesis 3–11 sketches more than 4,000 years of suffering that people experienced under the curse of sin.

But then God chose one man through whom He would resurrect His blessing for all mankind. God told this man, Abram, to leave his family, friends and everything else familiar to go "to the land which I will show you. . . . And in you all the families of the earth will be blessed" (Gen. 12:1,3). This promise ultimately found its fulfillment in Abram's descendant, Jesus Christ (see Matt. 1:1).

It staggers the mind that the hope of the world would come from God's promise to an elderly idol worshiper who, along with his wife, was well past childbearing years. In choosing Abram, God demonstrated grace. And in choosing to follow, Abram demonstrated faith.

Abram left Ur, a city with tremendous advantages. The move represented an incredible act of faith for Abram—especially for someone with no material needs. He forsook everything familiar to him to follow God into the unknown. And after he arrived in Canaan, he dwelt in a tent and struggled through famines in a barren land. It took faith for Abram to follow God—not just at the beginning, but every day.

God doesn't always lead by promotion. Neither does He seek our approval before He tells us to move on. In His grace, God chose Abram, who then responded in faith—and followed the Lord. The God of Abraham calls us to the same response today.

Jesus, son of Abraham, give me the faith of Abraham to leave everything to follow Your gracious leading. When the frustration of following seems too heavy, remind me that You called me by grace and that You offer me more blessing than Ur ever could.

It is the office of faith to believe what we do not see and . . . the reward of faith to see what we do believe. —*Thomas Adams*

See maps on pages 28-29, 56-57.

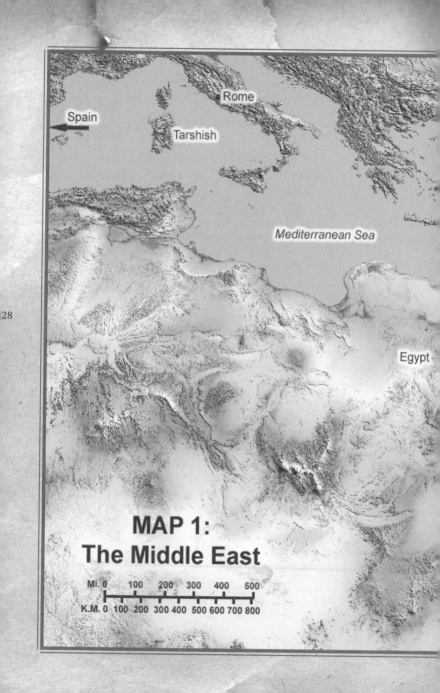

Spain

Rome

Tarshish

Mediterranean Sea

Egypt

MAP 1:
The Middle East

MI. 0   100   200   300   400   500

K.M. 0 100 200 300 400 500 600 700 800

A LOOK BELOW THE SURFACE

GENESIS 13:5-13

The Jordan Valley was well watered everywhere, "like the garden of the LORD" (Gen. 13:10), so Lot took his hungry flocks there. But choosing to dwell in the best of the land turned out to be one of the worst of decisions, for the text includes this ominous note: "This was before the LORD destroyed Sodom and Gomorrah" (v. 10). In fact, a glance ahead reveals that in addition to Sodom, God destroyed all vegetation in the land—the very reason why Lot initially felt attracted to the valley (see 19:25).

Here we acquire the painful principle that in time, we relinquish even the "benefits" of sin. What initially seemed so attractive to Lot— what so quickly satisfied his need—brought him what all fleshly decisions eventually bring: a temporary benefit with long-term regret (see 2 Pet. 2:7-8).

Consider how often we make lifelong choices based on the impulse of a glance. We buy cars with all the extras, we run stop signs, we date (or even marry) charming unbelievers, and we move to another city, only then to search for a good church. The questions we must ask ourselves are, *How will this decision affect me spiritually? How will this affect my relationship with God?*

Lot's failure teaches us that before we pay a penny for sin, we should consider the real price of a divided heart. Where we have compromised, we should immediately run to the forgiving arms of our Lord Jesus—and not look back.

Lord, help me remember that my spiritual life is my life—and that I am not my own. Give me eyes to see the spiritual implications of my decisions today.

If sin were not an ugly thing, would it wear a mask? . . . Truth is not ashamed of its name or nakedness; it can walk openly and boldly. —*George Swinnock*

See map on pages 98-99.

ALONG THE ROAD TO SHUR

GENESIS 16

For Sarai, the only thing worse than a barren land was a barren womb. So, turning to her culture's custom, she told her husband, Abram, to give her children through her Egyptian maid, Hagar. But when Hagar conceived, Sarai became resentful and mistreated Hagar, who then fled.

The Bible says that the Lord found Hagar "by a spring of water in the wilderness, by the spring on the way to Shur" (Gen. 16:7). The location reveals that Hagar intended to head back home—to Egypt. But God told her to return to Sarai and to name the child *Ishmael* (meaning, "God hears"), "for the LORD has heard of your misery" (v. 11, *NIV*). Hagar did so, and she called the Lord *El Roi*, "the God who sees me." The well by which she sat received the name *Beer Lahai Roi*, meaning, "the well of the Living One who sees me" (see vv. 13-14).

The meaning of the names "God hears" and "God sees" would remain constant reminders to Abram and his family. Earlier, Abram had run to Egypt to escape a famine in the land (see Gen. 12). Sarai had turned to an Egyptian to escape barrenness. Hagar had run to Egypt to escape misery. But each effort, apart from God, found them at the same place of having to trust Him all over again.

The Lord wants us to learn to turn to Him rather than run to Egypt during what seems inescapable despair. As we wait on the Lord, we have His promise that He waits with us, for *God hears* our prayers and *God sees* our needs.

O Lord, how often have I traveled the road to Shur toward some Egyptian decoy, running from a chance to trust You. In situations today when I feel like running, may You find me instead on my knees—before a God who hears and a God who sees.

If God told you on the front end how long you would wait . . . you'd lose heart. . . . But he doesn't. He just says, "Wait. I keep my word. . . . In the process of time I'm developing you to be ready." —*F. B. Meyer*

See maps on pages 28-29, 42-43, 98-99.

31

WORRY ON THE MOUNT

MATTHEW 6:25-34

Multitudes from all over Israel and her neighboring regions thronged to Galilee to see Jesus. He delivered His most famous sermon on a mount beside the northern shore of the Sea of Galilee. The traditional location of this sermon on the Mount of Beatitudes provides ample space for large crowds.

In springtime, the hillside bursts with grass and flowers. Jesus drew on this setting to illustrate simple truths to His listeners: "Do not be worried about your life . . . Look at the birds of the air . . . Observe how the lilies of the field grow" (Matt. 6:25-26,28). Jesus called the people, "You of little faith" (v. 30), because they sought tomorrow's needs instead of trusting God to provide for today's needs as He saw fit.

The real struggle for people (both then and now) seems to rest with control. For some reason, we feel more in control of our lives when we fret about them. But worry moves the burden of providing from God to us—a load that He never intended us to bear. When we seek first God's kingdom, we yield to His control of our lives. And we come to see all things—even working for food and clothing—as opportunities to promote God's kingdom and the growth of His righteousness in our hearts.

On a gentle slope in Galilee, Jesus used simple illustrations we also see in our land—birds, flowers and grass. God's continual care of these things gives testimony that He will provide for us too . . . as He always has.

Heavenly Father, thank You that Your promise to provide for me is not limited by my worries that You will. Help me remember that I cannot control the next five minutes, much less a thousand tomorrows. Today has enough trouble of its own, Lord, and so I give this day to You.

The beginning of anxiety is the end of faith. The beginning of true faith is the end of anxiety. —*George Muller*

See maps on pages 56-57, 70-71.

ON THE PATHS OF WISDOM

PROVERBS 2

The connection between the first steps we take in making a decision and its final outcome often seems disjointed. For example, in Proverbs 2, how does a lack of wisdom regarding adultery relate to the wicked being cut off from the land? What connection does the land have with morality?

The answer lies in verse 17: "[the immoral woman] forgets the covenant of her God." Adultery at the physical level reveals what has already begun at the spiritual level. The way one chooses to lead the spiritual life always has physical results. Not choosing wisely can have a domino effect that leads to far greater consequences than imaginable. No one better illustrates this than the primary author of Proverbs.

Solomon possessed the wisdom to govern all Israel, but he lacked the will to govern his own heart. His many wives introduced many gods to Israel—the beginnings of compromise that ultimately led to the nation's exile from the land. Solomon's wisdom could not override the effects of his defiance.

Certainly, a disciplined intake of Scripture promises wisdom. But wisdom offers a course of action, not just a course of instruction. The application of wisdom, or the lack thereof, always shows itself in life—for a man reaps what he sows (see Eccles. 12:13-14; Gal. 6:7-8).

Like a prophet, the book of Proverbs reveals the outcome of pathways chosen. It offers us hope as it looks to the desired end of our lives and challenges us to think backward along its logical course. How do we want our lives to end? In what areas must we succeed at all costs? The path we take today will lead us there.

> Lord, glancing back down the road I see many choices that led to where I am today, though at the time they seemed insignificant. Help me stay on the paths of wisdom today and so enjoy the benefits of wisdom tomorrow.

Life is like a day; it goes by so fast. If I am so careless with my days, how can I be careful with my life? —*Henri Nouwen*

See map on pages 56-57.

The ancient synagogue in Capernaum dates later than the first century, but it sits on the darker foundation from the time of Christ. Here, Jesus healed a man with an unclean spirit (see Day 4).

Worshipers praying at the Western Wall in Jerusalem. Note the scraps of paper between the stones on which people have written prayers (see Travelogue).

STARING DEATH IN THE FAITH

GENESIS 23:1-4; HEBREWS 11:8-16

Abraham lived for 62 years in the land God promised him before owning any of it. Even then, Abraham only purchased a plot of ground to bury his wife. The Cave of Machpelah in Hebron not only entombed Sarah's body, but it also became the burial place of Abraham, Isaac and Jacob.

So when Abraham purchased a plot to bury Sarah, he demonstrated great faith in God's promise to give him all the land—even though he (and many descendants) would die before ever receiving it. "All these died in faith, without receiving the promises," the book of Hebrews reminds us, "having confessed that they were strangers and exiles on the earth" (11:13). Even though we suffer great loss in death, we do not lose God's promises, because they continue beyond the grave.

We seem to be on an eternal quest for the good life in the here and now. Oh, we know about the hope of heaven and the bit about seeking first God's kingdom. But in spite of all we believe as true, we still scurry to find satisfaction in this life. When we fail to find it (as we always will), we often abandon the boring job, the struggling marriage or the imperfect church, believing that we've simply been looking in the wrong place. And in a way, we have.

Death brings the startling reality that this world is not our home. Like Abraham, we should remember that the ultimate satisfaction we seek comes after our death and resurrection. Death then represents not the end of life but its beginning.

Lord, help me not to seek all satisfaction here and now. But, like Christ, may I lay down my life, believing in all faith that I will take it up again—just as He did.

Let your hope of heaven master your fear of death. Why should you be afraid to die, who hopes to live by dying? —*William Gurnall*

See map on pages 98-99.

PEOPLE, PIGS AND PRIORITIES

MATTHEW 8:18-34

On one occasion, two Jews approached Jesus and declared they would follow Him wherever He went. But Jesus' response to them indicated that their hearts were more devoted to comfort and family than to Him (see Matt. 8:19-22).

After Jesus and His disciples sailed east across the Sea of Galilee, they landed at modern Kursi in "the country of the Gadarenes" (Matt. 8:28). But Mark and Luke use a more general location, citing "the country of the Gerasenes" (Mark 5:1; Luke 8:26), referring to the city of Gerasa (modern Jerash), a large, Greco-Roman city some miles away from the eastern shore.

After landing in this Gentile territory, Jesus immediately encountered two men possessed by a legion of demons and cast them out of the men and into a herd of swine. When the pigs plunged down the steep hillside into the lake and drowned, the entire town "implored Him to leave their region" (Matt. 8:34). The people felt more concern over the loss of their livelihood than the restoration of the men who were possessed. Like the Jews across the lake, these Gentiles held other things as more important than following Jesus.

While we probably would never admit to having a higher priority in pigs than in people, our commitments to comfort and even to our family often betray a devotion that sinks to the same level (see Luke 14:26). To love the Lord with all our heart means that Christ should have no rivals in our life. So as we follow Christ today, let us commit to nothing before our devotion to Him—whether creature comforts, livelihood, fear or even family ties.

Lord Jesus, as I left everything to follow You at the beginning, so I hold nothing as dear as You now. If today challenges me to fear or to focus my heart elsewhere, I will remember that with a simple word You calmed the sea and made dark spirits flee. You alone are God.

Discipleship is anything that causes what is believed in the heart to have demonstrable consequences in our daily life. —*Eugene Peterson*

See maps on pages 56-57, 70-71.

AT LAST . . . ROOM FOR US

GENESIS 26:12-22

Israel's first prime minister, David Ben-Gurion, saw the vast expanse of Israel's Negev as something that offered great potential. In 1953, he settled in the kibbutz *Sede Boker*, urging Israelis to help him tame the Negev into a new society. Initially, the idea seemed no more than a pipe dream.

In the Negev, life has one uncompromising requirement: water. So, in the book of Genesis, when the Philistines spitefully filled in Isaac's wells, he dug more. The first two wells he named "Argument" and "Opposition," because herdsmen in the land claimed the water rights for themselves (see Gen. 26:19-21). But the third well posed no problem, so he named it "Room Enough," saying, "At last the LORD has made room for us" (v. 22). Isaac sowed in the Negev and reaped a hundredfold during the same year. The text reveals how he could do it: "The LORD blessed him" (v. 12). Nothing could stop God from fulfilling His promises to Abraham and his descendants—not a desolate land or even contentious neighbors—and nothing can stop Him from fulfilling His promises to us.

Today, the small home where Ben-Gurion lived in the Negev houses a museum memorializing his dream. And water piped south from Galilee has helped bring his dream to life. Even the birth of the state of Israel in 1948 affirms God's faithfulness to continue with a people who will receive the land promised to Abraham. Isaac's words almost sound prophetic: "At last the LORD has made room for us, and we will be fruitful in the land" (v. 22).

> Lord, I've lost count of the wells that the Philistines have filled in my life. It seems every bit of progress I enjoy finds the enemy in opposition. But Your care for Isaac in the barren Negev and Your sustaining the Jews throughout the ages reveal that You are a God who keeps His word. A thousand lost wells only serve to glorify You more when You fulfill Your promises to me against impossible odds.

There is a living God; He has spoken in the Bible. He means what He says and will do all He has promised. —*Hudson Taylor*

See maps on pages 56-57, 98-99.

GOD'S GATEWAY

GENESIS 28:11-19; JOHN 1:43-51

In his flight to Haran, Jacob spent the night at Bethel, where years earlier his grandfather Abraham had heard God promise that he would receive all the land as far as he could see. There, Jacob dreamed of a stairway to heaven, and the Lord repeated to him the promises that Abraham received.

Shaken, Jacob awoke and cried, "How awesome is this place! This is none other than the house of God, and this is the gate of heaven" (Gen. 28:17). So at the place where Abraham built an altar in worship, Jacob responded in kind and named the site *Bethel* —"house of God." Jacob never forgot the place, for even on his deathbed he told his sons how God Almighty appeared to him there and promised to give the land to Jacob's descendants for an everlasting possession (see Gen. 48:3-4).

Jacob's sons became the 12 tribes of Israel, and centuries later they re-entered and took this land. Their first victory after Jericho occurred in the region of Bethel and Ai—the very place where centuries before God had promised the land to Jacob. Thus, Bethel became not merely Jacob's "gate of heaven" but also Israel's gateway into the land they would inherit.

Many centuries later, the Lord Jesus would tell Nathaniel, "You will see the heavens opened and the angels of God ascending and descending on the Son of Man" (John 1:51). Jesus became the new Bethel, God's dwelling place. By comparing Himself to Jacob's ladder, Jesus revealed that God's means of communicating with mankind would now come through His Son—a means and a mediator that we still enjoy today (see Heb. 1:1-2; 7:25).

Lord Jesus, just as Bethel became Israel's gateway into Abraham's land, so You became the gateway into Abraham's blessing. Indeed, You are "the gate" by which all Israelites—even anyone who believes in You—may come to God [see John 10:9].

[Jesus is a gate] narrow and hard in the entrance, yet, after we have entered, wide and glorious. —*Thomas Adams*

See maps on pages 28-29, 84-85, 98-99.

A POINT OF COMPARISON

MATTHEW 10:5-15

The infamy of Sodom and Gomorrah lies buried in the words "sodomy" and "sodomites," which reflect the sin of Sodom and those who engaged in it. The twin cities never rose again to be habitable after their violent destruction in Genesis, yet we find their names recurring from Genesis to Revelation. These icons of decadence—referred to by Moses, the prophets, Jesus and the writers of the New Testament—came to represent the epitome of man's evil and God's response to it.

Imagine, then, the force behind Jesus' statement to His disciples that if a city refused to accept their teaching, "it will be more tolerable for the land of Sodom and Gomorrah in the day of judgment than for that city" (Matt. 10:15). Jesus sent His disciples to preach the message that He and John the Baptist gave earlier: "Repent, for the Kingdom of Heaven is at hand" (3:2; 4:17). Israel's long expectation of the Kingdom should have produced their acceptance of the King. But instead, city after city rejected Christ. This is why Jesus would later tell the people of Capernaum, "It will be more tolerable for the land of Sodom in the day of judgment, than for you" (11:23-24).

Jesus' repeated comparison of Sodom and Israel reveals that the only thing more tragic than sin is refusing its remedy. Christ removed the threat of judgment for us by taking our sin upon Himself through His death on the cross. Yet, we still learn that with greater revelation comes greater responsibility. Christ never intended His teachings to make us smarter sinners, but so that we might obey all that He has commanded us (see 28:18-20).

Lord Jesus, You have blessed me with an abundance of revelation—all of it, in fact, in the pages of Scripture. Help me embrace this book as more than devotional material that makes me feel better about myself. May Your words move past my mind and my checklist to my hands, my heart and my mouth. May I apply Your words as the life-changing agent You intended when You first spoke them beside the Sea of Galilee.

Duty is ours; consequences are God's. —*Stonewall Jackson*

See maps on pages 70-71, 98-99.

GOD'S CAMP

GENESIS 32:1-10

Returning from Haran to the land of Canaan forced Jacob to face a problem he had run from 20 years earlier—his deception of his brother Esau. As he approached the border of Canaan, angels of God came to meet him. The phrase "angels of God" appears only twice in the whole Old Testament: earlier at Bethel when Jacob left the land, and here, as he returned. After seeing the angels, Jacob named the place *Mahanaim*, saying, "This is God's camp" (Gen. 32:2).

The names Jacob gave the two sites reflected the momentous connection between them. *Bethel* means "House of God," while *Mahanaim* probably best means "God's camp." When Jacob learned that Esau was approaching with an army of 400 men, he did what every believer should do in a time of fear—he prayed. But after his "amen," Jacob retreated again to his own devices and sent gifts ahead to placate Esau's wrath.

41

The angels of God who appeared at critical moments in Jacob's life remind us that "our struggle is not against flesh and blood" (Eph. 6:12). We face a spiritual battle today, not merely a physical one. As such, we must fight on the spiritual level—with prayer and dependence on God—and not with our own wits or wealth.

The event at Mahanaim reveals that God's presence is with us long before our struggles arrive. It reveals His willingness to give spiritual victory in our physical lives when we bow before Him in weakness. As we face each day, we can know in faith: "This is God's camp."

Lord, it really all comes down to this: Will I trust that You are with me and are Lord of all or will I, in fear, try to seize control myself? I come to You in dependent prayer today, Lord, knowing that this is my only weapon . . . and my only defense.

No one prays for anything who has not been deeply alarmed.
—*Martin Luther*

See maps on pages 28-29, 56-57, 84-85.

MAP 2:
Egypt and Sinai

MI. 0   20   40   60
K.M. 0   25   50   75

Nile River

Gulf of Su

42

Jerusalem

Kadesh Barnea

Wilderness of Zin

lderness
of Shur

SINAI

43

Rephidim

Mount Sinai?
(Horeb)

Gulf of Aqaba

Red Sea

STRUGGLING WITH GOD

GENESIS 32:24-30

In the Bible, when God changed a person's name, He also changed the person. And with Jacob, the change took a brawl. After a desperate Jacob sent his family and possessions on across the Jabbok River, he remained alone as he anticipated meeting his brother, Esau. Instead he faced God—in the form of a man—and wrestled with Him until a mere touch from the Man wrenched Jacob's hip from its socket. "Let me go, for the dawn is breaking," the Man said. But Jacob replied, "I will not let you go unless you bless me" (Gen. 32:26).

Asking Jacob his name elicited nothing less than a confession, for *Jacob* means "heel-catcher" or "deceiver." Having confessed, Jacob could then be blessed. "Your name shall no longer be Jacob," the Man said, "but Israel [meaning "God fights for" or "contends against"]; for you have striven with God and with men and have prevailed" (v. 28). Jacob, now renamed, called the place where the change had occurred *Peniel*. The name means "God's face," revealing Jacob's insight into the significance of the event.

Jacob encountered God face to face, and it changed him. He learned that his manipulative, deceiving ways did not hold the means of getting God's blessing. Yes, God determined to bless Jacob, but first He determined that Jacob surrender his will. And in so doing, God told him he prevailed.

God may wrestle with us for a time—years, perhaps—and at any moment finish the struggle with one crushing touch. These excruciating events in our lives represent His grace, for in the pain He means not to destroy us but to compel us to change—that He may bless us.

> God of Jacob, every struggle I take up with You really stems from a struggle to surrender. You are in complete control; I am not. You are God; I am not, and there is no other. I seek Your face today, Lord, with all my heart.

What does this world need: gifted men and women, outwardly empowered? Or individuals who are broken, inwardly transformed?
—*Gene Edwards*

See map on pages 84-85.

YOUR HOLY HILL

PSALM 15

After David conquered Jerusalem and secured it as his capital, he desired to bring the Ark of the Covenant into his new City of David. But in his passion to have God's presence, David neglected to follow God's principles, and that negligence of improperly transporting the Ark cost a man his life (see 2 Sam. 6:1-7). Three months later, David correctly transported the Ark into Jerusalem and placed it in a tent he pitched for its keeping.

David gained a profound respect for God's holiness. His opening question in Psalm 15 reflects this awe: "O LORD, who may abide in Your tent? Who may dwell on Your holy hill?" (v. 1). David's answer ought to humble every reader: Only holy people may approach a holy God. The implications soon become clear: If only the holy may approach God's holy hill, then no one may come—for all fall short of God's perfection. The single possibility of approaching God comes from His grace in removing the impenetrable obstacle: our sin.

No one has ever entered God's presence without a sacrifice for sin, either then or now. God Himself offered the perfect sacrifice when His Son, Jesus, died on a cross in Jerusalem. Christ's sacrifice removed the obstacle of sin and imputes God's standard of holiness to those who would receive it by faith in Jesus.

It's not enough simply to believe in God and live as sincerely as we can. God is holy, and the place He resides is holy. As David learned, desiring God remains inadequate unless we approach Him as He prescribes (see John 14:6).

One who was sinless ascended to Jerusalem and bled on its soil for my sin. So through the blood of Jesus that makes me holy, pure, and wholly yours, I enter Your presence, Lord, to worship on Your holy hill.

Before I begin to think and consider the love of God and the mercy and compassion of God, I must start with the Holiness of God.
—*Martin Lloyd-Jones*

See map on page 112.

NATURAL FEATURES

GENESIS 37:12-28

Jacob's 10 oldest sons had traveled north to pasture their father Jacob's flocks at Shechem. So Jacob dispatched Joseph, whom he loved more than all his other sons, from the Valley of Hebron to check on their welfare. When Joseph arrived, he found that his brothers had moved farther north to the lush pastures of Dothan. Seeing him in the distance, the brothers—jealous of their father's love for Joseph—purposed to kill the boy. But the presence of a nearby cistern convinced them instead to hurl Joseph into it—and leave him there to die.

Providentially, the international highway that ran from Syria to Egypt split three ways as it snaked through the Mount Carmel range. One of these passes ran through Dothan, right where the brothers were. So when they noticed a caravan of Ishmaelite traders taking their wares to Egypt, they decided to sell Joseph as a slave rather than to kill him.

The Lord used the natural features of the land as a part of His supernatural plan for Joseph's life. The lushness of Dothan, the nearby cistern, the timely caravan headed south on an international highway—all natural elements of a marvelous plan that God blended together to produce His blessing.

Looking at our own lives, we often only see a flat tire, an angry parent, and an unfair job dismissal. In our pain, we can easily misinterpret God's dealings as unfair—or even cruel—when in fact He intends them to benefit us beyond our dreams. We glorify God when we worship Him in our confusion, trusting a wise heavenly Father who uses each event for our good and for His glory.

> Sovereign God, You waste no experience in my life. All fit tightly within the workings of Your will—which I can never comprehend. As Paul exclaimed, so do I: "Oh, the depth of the riches both of the wisdom and knowledge of God! How unsearchable are His judgments and unfathomable His ways!" (Rom. 11:33).

Judge not the Lord by feeble sense. But trust Him for His grace; Behind a frowning providence He hides a smiling face. —*William Cowper*

See maps on pages 28-29, 70-71, 84-85, 98-99.

46

THAT THE TRUTH MAY TAKE ROOT

MATTHEW 13:1-15

The event of Jesus teaching a large crowd from a boat most likely occurred at a small cove along the north shore of the Sea of Galilee. One study revealed that about 14,000 people could fit on a hillside located there and still hear a lone voice from the cove below. Within this natural theater, Jesus taught the people.

In Matthew 12:22-29, when Jesus healed people in Capernaum, the religious leaders attributed His miracles to Satan. Up to that point, Jesus' message had offered Israel the long-awaited kingdom of God, but now He realized that Israel would reject His offer. So, by speaking in parables, Jesus shifted His message from preparing the nation for the Kingdom to preparing the disciples for the Church.

"That day," Matthew notes, "[Jesus] spoke many things to them in parables" (Matt. 13:1,3). When Jesus' disciples asked Him why the change, Jesus answered that parables served to reveal truth to those willing to receive it—and to conceal the truth from those unwilling. Jesus' parable of the sower who scattered seed on various soils represented the various responses to God's Word—from the hard heart that ignores the truth to the soft heart that hears and applies it.

But the story also calls each of us to examine our own personal response to the Bible. Do we truly listen to God's Word in order for God to change us? Do our hearts long to bear fruit for the Lord? Or like the throng along the shore that day, do we just gather to hear stories from a gifted teacher?

Lord, pull the thorns, rake the rocks and cultivate my hard heart until the truth takes root in a life eager to glorify You. Let me not waste the seed You scatter on my heart by failing to apply what I clearly hear You saying.

Distance from God is a frightening thing. God will never adjust His agenda to fit ours. He will not speed His pace to catch up with ours; we need to slow *our* pace in order to recover our walk with Him.
—Charles R. Swindoll

See map on pages 70-71.

The Temple Mount in Jerusalem outlines the same dimensions as it did during the time of Christ (see Day 36).

The hill to the left slopes up about 60 degrees from the Kidron Valley and provided Jerusalem excellent protection from the east. To the right sits the Mount of Olives, the place of Christ's ascension and His Second Coming (see Day 39).

IN THIS LAND OF MY AFFLICTION

GENESIS 41:51–42:5

Joseph gave his sons Hebrew names, which revealed his continued faith in God despite his difficult years spent in Egypt. In naming his firstborn "Manasseh," Joseph gave God credit as the One who had made him forget the toil and the pain his family had brought him (see Gen. 41:51). Joseph's second son he called "Ephraim," meaning "fruitfulness," for Joseph said, "God has made me fruitful in the land of my affliction" (v. 52).

But Egypt would become a land of affliction for more than just Joseph. The dreams that Joseph had interpreted for Pharaoh meant that God intended to follow seven years of plenty in the land with seven years of famine on the land—a disaster the Nile's generous water supply could not rise above. Just as God earlier used natural elements to bring Joseph to Egypt, so the Lord would use the same to bring all nations to Joseph.

The famine spread to Canaan, and in order to get food, Joseph's brothers had to travel the same highway to Egypt by which they had sent Joseph 22 years earlier. God purposed to make the brothers fruitful (like Joseph) in a land of suffering, but not before He first developed faithfulness in them such as Joseph had displayed.

Just as the thread of sovereignty continued to weave through the family of Joseph, so God loops His needle through our lives and draws us close to Him. We must remember in our struggles that our duty lies outside of trying to understand God's plan. He never asks that of us. Instead, He wants to see our trust in Him, through simple daily obedience, even in a land of affliction and confusion.

> *Lord, both pain and prosperity demand that I bow before You in humility, trust and dependence. My heart longs for faithfulness, Lord, not certain circumstances. Give me the faith of Joseph and the maturity to love and obey You in spite of today's worst events.*

Faithfulness in carrying out present duties is the best preparation for the future. —*Francis Fenelon*

See maps on pages 28-29, 42-43, 56-57.

OUT OF CONTROL

GENESIS 42:38–43:10

Before Joseph would allow his brothers to purchase any more grain, he required them to bring to him the very person that Jacob had refused to release into God's control—his youngest son, Benjamin. When the brothers reported this to their father, Jacob clung to Benjamin, saying, "My son shall not go down with you" (Gen. 42:38).

However, like straws loaded on a camel's back, day after parched day of the famine finally took their toll. "If it must be so," Jacob conceded, "take your brother also, and arise, return to the man" (43:11,13). The circumstances literally forced him to do what he refused to do otherwise: trust God with his sons.

Judah had reminded his father that they could have gone to Egypt and returned twice in the time it was taking Jacob to surrender Benjamin. Two round trips from Hebron to Egypt amounted to about 1,000 miles—or seven weeks hard travel. Jacob wasted seven weeks, only to find himself facing the same issue as he faced in the beginning.

Problems never just go away or take care of themselves, especially when God allows them in order to shape our character. God will patiently wait and allow the circumstances to compel us to do what we should have done at the beginning: surrender all control to God.

We should hold nothing as dear to us as trust in God—not money, not a position, not even a child. Ultimately, comfort cannot come from a hope that God will protect us from pain. Our comfort can only come from trusting that God remains in complete control for His good purposes—even in what seems the worst of circumstances.

Father, prayer is more than asking of You, but surrendering to You as well. So I surrender all control to You right now. Help me not waste precious time, as Jacob did, by refusing to trust You with even my most precious possessions, positions or persons.

From the example of Jacob let us learn patient endurance, should the Lord often compel us, by pressure of circumstances, to do many things contrary to the inclination of our own minds. —*John Calvin*

See maps on pages 28-29, 98-99.

FOR THOSE IN PERIL ON THE SEA

MATTHEW 14:25-32

Jesus performed more miracles in the vicinity of the Sea of Galilee than any other place in His ministry. Standing on its shores, one can easily see across the shallow lake, which measures about 7 by 13 miles. The hills to the east and west tower above the water.

As cool air from these heights rushes down the slopes into the lake's warmer basin, winds can whip up the surface of the water to deadly proportions. A small craft, such as the one Matthew reported the disciples clung to during a stormy night, could find itself foundering in an instant. To make matters worse, when the disciples saw Jesus walking on the water, they thought He was a ghost!

But Jesus told them, "Take courage, it is I; do not be afraid" (Matt. 14:27). Peter replied, "Lord, if it is You, command me to come to You on the water" (v. 28). Jesus said, "Come." And so, Peter did.

Almost as incredible as Peter's walking on the water was Jesus' rebuke when Peter sank. Peter was the only other person besides Christ to ever walk on the waves, and Jesus told him he had little faith! Why? Because Peter had little faith compared to what he knew. Just hours earlier on the shore, Jesus had given Peter and the disciples an equally impossible task in feeding the 5,000: "You give them something to eat" (v. 16). And they did . . . through the enabling provision of Jesus.

That day, Christ taught His disciples—in a variety of locations—a single truth we also should never forget: We must come to Him not only by requesting provision, but also by stepping out of the boat in faith, believing that He has provided all we need to obey Him.

> Lord, help me to apply in all contexts the faithfulness I display in just a few. I know the tempest I face today is but an opportunity for You to reveal Your faithful character—and to develop mine.

I need to be continually sensitive to the surprising places where God can meet me. —*Charles Killian*

See map on pages 70-71.

A MOVING EXPERIENCE

GENESIS 46:1-5

The refrain "from sea to shining sea" in the song "America the Beautiful" refers to the east-west borders of the United States. In a similar way, in ancient Israel, the phrase "from Dan to Beersheba" practically described all of Israel from north to south.

When Jacob came to Beersheba, leaving Canaan on his way to Egypt, a wave of emotion undoubtedly washed over the old man. Jacob's grandfather Abraham had given the city its name. Jacob's father, Isaac, had also sojourned in Beersheba, raising Jacob and his brother, Esau, there. From there, Jacob had last seen his mother, Rebekah, as he fled from his brother's anger.

For 130 years, Jacob associated Beersheba with everything familiar—and with memories of home. So, as Jacob left the land that would span from Dan to Beersheba—the land promised to Abraham, Isaac and Jacob—God spoke words of comfort to the patriarch. God's words to Jacob remain a promise to all the fearful whom He leads. Read them slowly: "I am God . . . do not be afraid to go . . . I will make you a great nation there. I will go down with you" (Gen. 46:3-4).

So often in our lives, God's leading produces fear in us because it requires us to journey from the familiar to the unknown. But the One who is God offers peace of mind to those who will trust Him (see Isa. 26:3). He reminds us that His blessings lie where He wants to take us, not in our clinging to the familiar. And, most beautifully, He promises to go with us.

53

Lord Jesus, You gave me a promise that Jacob also received: "I will be with you always." And so I will not be afraid to follow You into a future that I can't see—even to the ends of the earth.

Never be afraid to trust an unknown future to a known God.
—*Corrie ten Boom*

See maps on pages 28-29, 56-57, 70-71, 98-99.

THE VALUE OF DAILY OBEDIENCE

GENESIS 49:1-10

Jacob's firstborn, Reuben, attempted to prematurely seize the role of his father by having relations with his father's concubine. This role was due him as the firstborn, but by taking too soon what would be his, he lost it all. "Uncontrolled as water," Jacob said to him, "you shall not have preeminence [any longer], because you went up to your father's bed; then you defiled it" (Gen. 49:4).[1]

Similarly, Simeon and Levi took matters into their own hands when they were wronged and—rather than waiting on God to avenge them—murdered the men of Shechem. All three sons tried to force God's will before God's timing. So the blessing usually given to the firstborn passed over these three and rested on the fourth son, Judah—from whom came the Savior of the world.

54

Centuries later, these sons' sins would also affect their tribes' inheritance in the Promised Land. Jacob foretold that Simeon's and Levi's descendants would be scattered throughout the nation of Israel (see v. 7). In time, Simeon's tribe found its land swallowed up by Judah, and the priestly tribe of Levi was scattered throughout the tribes with no inheritance but the Lord. And, like their ancestor, the tribe of Reuben presumed to receive God's blessing prematurely by settling east of the Jordan—outside the borders of the land God originally intended. Ultimately, none of these three tribes could point to any portion of the true Promised Land as their own.

For us, the sons underscore the value of daily, patient obedience to the Lord. Our actions will affect not only our future—and the future of our children—but also potentially the blessing the world may receive through us in Christ. Trying to snatch God's will before God's timing amounts to missing God's will altogether.

> Father, help me today not to take the easy route of compromise and impatient ambition. Help me wed my privilege as Your son with an unwavering patience in Your perfect timing.

Nothing is really lost by a life of sacrifice; everything is lost by failure to obey God's call. —Henry P. Liddon

See maps on pages 56-57, 98-99.

WE BEHELD HIS GLORY

MATTHEW 16:13–17:9

Jesus' preparation of the disciples for the age of the Church included teaching them that He would die in Jerusalem and rise again (see Matt. 16:21). On the heels of this unthinkable statement, He made another just as fantastic: "If anyone wishes to come after Me, he must deny himself, and take up his cross and follow Me" (v. 24). The cross exposed the disciples' expectations: their own privileged positions in the Kingdom. But Jesus said discipleship also included the obligation to crucify selfish desires.

Christ didn't remove the hope of His kingdom; He simply relegated it to its proper place. Six days later, Jesus took Peter, James and John from the region of Caesarea Philippi to a "high mountain," probably the nearby snow-capped Mount Hermon (see 17:1). There, Jesus' appearance changed. His face shone like the sun and His clothes became dazzling white—a sight made even more glorious with the snow.

These scenes, side by side, seemed a wild contradiction—Jesus' death and Jesus' glory. But Christ revealed these extremes so that one might strengthen the other. He provided assurance of His coming Kingdom to the disciples He had commanded to take up their cross in the meantime (see 1 Pet. 5:1,10).

As with the disciples, the cross reveals our expectations. How do we respond to the harsh reality of self-sacrifice? Only the promise of heaven provides the stamina to follow a crucified Savior and to put our selfish ambition aside. We can shoulder our cross today only by scaling the mountain and gazing on the glory of One who bore the cross before us . . . and for us.

Lord Jesus, may the cross I bear today not obscure my destination. Thank You for showing me Your glory so that I may have strength and hope for the hard journey home.

To live without hope is to cease to live. —*Fyodor Dostoevsky*

See map on pages 70-71.

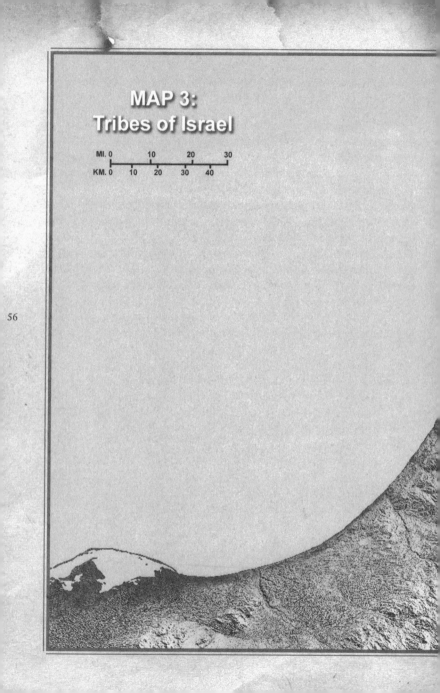

MAP 3:
Tribes of Israel

MI. 0   10   20   30
KM. 0   10   20   30   40

56

DAN

ASHER

NAPHTALI

ZEBULUN

ISSACHAR

M A N A S S E H

57

EPHRAIM

GAD

N

BENJAMIN

JUDAH

REUBEN

IMEON

ON HOLY GROUND

EXODUS 3:1-8

In Hebrew, Adam's name means "man," and it relates to the word "adamah," meaning "ground," from which God formed him. Accordingly, when Adam sinned, God cursed the ground to which Adam would return when he died.

It seems surprising, then, that the first use of the noun form "holy" in the Hebrew Bible finds its connection with the ground: "Remove your sandals," God told Moses at Horeb, "for the place on which you are standing is holy ground" (Exod. 3:5). Although the ground itself held no intrinsic value, God's presence there with Moses sanctified the ground—set it apart—from all other places. Later, when Moses constructed a tabernacle for God to dwell in among His people, the designations "holy place" and "most holy place" referred to the proximity of God's presence. And the command God gave to the Israelites to "be holy" reflected His own holiness (see Lev. 20:26).

When God called Moses from the burning bush, the Lord promised to lead His people out of Egypt "to a good and spacious land" (Exod. 3:8). But He also purposed to make them holy—just as He does us. Paul noted, "The first man [Adam] is from the earth, earthy; the second man [Christ] is from heaven [and] just as we have borne the image of the earthy, we will also bear the image of the heavenly" (1 Cor. 15:47,49).

God displays His grace in that He can take the ordinary—whether a people or a piece of ground—and make it holy. God can even take something He cursed—the ground, mankind, even all creation—and sanctify it through the shed blood of Jesus.

> God, just as You breathed life into Adam, one formed from dust, You have done the same in me—and not just physically. For You who said, "Light shall shine out of darkness" have made to shine in my heart the "light of the knowledge of the glory of God" (2 Cor. 4:6-7). Thank You for glorifying Yourself today through the earthen vessel of my life.

Holiness . . . is something we are to do because of what we already are.
—C. S. Lewis

See maps on pages 28-29, 42-43.

PURE WATER

PROVERBS 5:15-23

When the Hebrews lived along the great rivers of Mesopotamia and Egypt, the need for water never posed a problem. But when God led His people into Canaan, they quickly discovered that their lives depended on rain, not rivers—and that rain came from God. Even the local Canaanites looked to the supernatural for water by worshiping Baal, the so-called god of rain.

For God's people, then, faithfulness to Him held the key to blessing—even survival. He called the worship of other gods—and the belief that they provided water for life—spiritual adultery (see Ezek. 23:37).

The Lord used this powerful image to communicate the need for purity in marriage. In Proverbs 5, the thirst for water is compared to sensual desire. Using the metaphors of a cistern, a well and a spring, God revealed that the source from which one drinks brings life or death.

The image presents infidelity as wasteful—"Should your springs overflow in the streets?" (Prov. 5:16, *NIV*)—and unnecessary, for God gives a man all he needs within his own marriage. In fact, God directs him always to "be exhilarated" with his wife, or literally, "intoxicated," which intensifies the drinking metaphor (v. 19). Ultimately, the passage relates acts of passion to spiritual choices and consequences, "For the ways of a man are before the eyes of the LORD" (v. 21).

God's people never needed to look beyond the Lord for all the pure water they needed. So God's people need not look outside of marriage to slake the thirst that God created marriage to satisfy.

Lord, the culture offers many sensual idols that promise fulfillment but deliver death. Thank You for revealing these lies. Thank You for Your perfect provision.

There is no more lovely, friendly or charming relationship, communion or company, than a good marriage. —*Martin Luther*

See maps on pages 28-29, 56-57.

THE LIFEBLOOD OF EGYPT

EXODUS 7:14-18

The power of Egypt spanned millennia. In fact, more years of biblical history occurred in Egypt than in any other nation outside of the land of Israel. The sole source of Egypt's strength flowed 4,000 miles long—the longest river in the world.

The Nile represented the lifeblood of Egypt. Without its vital supply, Egypt would have been a mere desert in North Africa. The river flooded its banks annually, providing the land a rich silt perfectly suited for farming. Because the flood occurred the same time each year, the Nile determined Egypt's calendar. The Egyptians deified the great river as a god, whose spirit they called "Hapi," and whose waters they considered the bloodstream of Osiris, the god of the underworld.

Therefore, when God turned the Nile to blood in the first plague of the Exodus, He not only wounded the heart of Egyptian sustenance but also struck the Egyptian gods by revealing them as powerless. Over and over in Exodus, God provided both disaster and deliverance to communicate that He, and no other, was the Lord (see 6:7-8; 7:5,17; 10:2; 14:4,18; 16:12).

The world offers numerous distractions from the true source of our sustenance and success. God never intended the consistent means of our provision to replace our dependence on Him. From the reliability of the seasons, to the food always ready at the market, to the automatic deposits that appear in our accounts, all we have flows from God's gracious hand (see Neh. 2:18; 6:16; Jas. 1:17). And He can remove it in a moment to remind us it is so.

Mighty God, what great rivers am I trusting in today apart from You? In this moment of awareness, I ask You to reveal them as powerless. Open my eyes to realize You alone are God . . . and the very lifeblood of my existence each day.

The world forgets you, its creator, and falls in love with what you have created instead of with you. —*Augustine of Hippo*

See maps on pages 28-29, 42-43.

OPEN UP, ANCIENT GATES!

PSALM 24; LUKE 18:18-27

The Scriptures teach that when the Messiah descends, His feet will stand on the Mount of Olives east of Jerusalem and He will judge the nations (see Zech. 14:4). Scattered along that hillside today, thousands of Jewish graves give testimony to the hope that those buried there will receive a more benevolent resurrection when Messiah comes.

One tradition states that after Jesus descends, He will enter Jerusalem through the Golden Gate, which lies just across the valley from the Mount of Olives. Because of this tradition, centuries ago Christian opponents bricked the gate closed, hoping to deter the Messiah's arrival, and they placed their own graveyard before the gate in order to ritually defile anyone who would enter.

In Psalm 24, David poses a profound question: "Who may ascend into the hill of the LORD? And who may stand in His holy place?" (v. 3). A weighty answer follows: "He who has clean hands and a pure heart" (v. 4). In other words, nobody.

"No one is good except God alone," Jesus would later confirm (Luke 18:19). Yet while no one measures up to God's standard, "The things that are impossible with people are possible with God" (v. 27). One can only approach God by His grace—not by religious deeds, prayers or even a strategic interment on the Mount of Olives.

Someday, what David proclaimed will occur: "Open up, ancient gates! . . . and let the King of glory enter" (Ps. 24:7, *NLT*). When that day comes, no bricked gate will hinder the King of glory. Even more amazing, no sin will hinder those who come to God by grace through faith in the Lord Jesus, the Messiah.

Lord Jesus, You will enter Jerusalem again—and I will be behind You. Thank You for the grace that cleansed my hands and heart and flung open the ancient gates of justice that barred me from Your holy place.

Grace teaches us that God loves because of who God is, not because of who we are. —*Philip Yancey*

See map on page 112.

These ancient olive trees in the Garden of Gethsemane most likely weren't the ones that beheld Christ in prayer (Roman legions cut down Jerusalem's trees in their siege on the city in A.D. 70). However, these trees may have grown from the stumps that remained (see Day 40).

The Hinnom Valley in Jerusalem, in the days of Judah's kings, was the site of horrific acts of idol worship and child sacrifice. Jesus used this valley as an illustration of hell. In fact, we get the word "hell" from its name in Greek: *Gehenna* (see Day 42).

ACTS OF GOD

EXODUS 10:14-23

In Egypt, the plagues probably began in August when the Nile flooded and lasted until Passover in April. After the seventh plague, when hail destroyed crops and cattle, Pharaoh's court officials asked him, "Do you not realize that Egypt is destroyed?" (Exod. 10:7).

The subsequent swarm of locusts—which typically average 130 million locusts per square mile—"ate every plant of the land" (v. 15). And if the plague of darkness "which may be felt" (v. 21) included a violent sandstorm (known as the *Khamsin*), it would mean the Lord had used the land itself to contribute to the plagues' terror and economic devastation. The horrific destruction stands in even broader relief when we read that in nearby Goshen, where the Israelites lived, the land remained unaffected (see 9:26).

In a world in which God's common grace allows the rain to fall on the just and the unjust, the lines between Goshen and Egypt—or believers and unbelievers—are not always clearly defined. When natural disasters (or "acts of God") devastate all lives in their wake regardless of people's faith, it can seem difficult to understand the distinction God made in ancient Egypt.

God's unhurried methods of bringing about justice speak to His patience, not His apathy or inability (see 2 Pet. 3:9). The destruction of Egypt and the protection of Goshen stand as miniscule examples of what God will one day bring about on a cosmic scale. These examples stand as a warning to all unbelievers and as an encouragement to all of us who believe (see 2 Pet. 2:9).

> *Lord, I stand in awe of Your workings in the world—often extraordinary in scale and mystifying in purpose. My mind struggles to fathom how the force of a hurricane embodies but a whisper of Your power. Thank You for the justice You will bring about one day and for the grace that set me in Goshen.*

The greatest single distinguishing feature of the omnipotence of God is that our imagination gets lost thinking about it. —*Blaise Pascal*

See maps on pages 28-29, 42-43.

64

A HOUSE OF UNRIPE FIGS

MATTHEW 21:1-19

The road that Jesus walked from Jericho to Jerusalem for His final Passover passed through Bethany and Bethphage at the southeastern slope of the Mount of Olives, just east of Jerusalem. As Jesus approached Bethphage (whose name means "house of unripe figs"), He directed two of His disciples to retrieve a donkey on which He would enter Jerusalem—to the contempt of the Jewish leaders.

When Jesus entered the Temple area, He found the Court of the Gentiles, the area for Gentiles to worship God, filled with markets and money changers. Jesus promptly cleaned house, saying, "It is written, 'My house shall be called a house of prayer;' but you are making it a 'robber's den'" (Matt. 21:13).

The next morning, Jesus returned to Jerusalem along the same road He had traveled before and saw a fig tree in leaf, which typically indicated that it would have unripe figs. But the tree offered only leaves. Jesus cursed the tree—not in a fit of anger, but in order to represent what He saw the day before in the Jewish leaders and the Temple: There was no fruit present when all indications suggested otherwise.

A few days later, Jesus would tell His disciples that He chose them for a particular reason: "That you would go and bear fruit, and that your fruit would remain" (John 15:16). Jesus desires the same for us.

The lives of the religious always bear leaves but not always unripe figs. When Jesus looks at our lives, He expects to find our faith lived out in authenticity. He wants to find us fruitful. In fact, that's why He chose us.

65

> *Lord Jesus, You are the vine and I am the branch who must remain in You to bear fruit [see John 15:5,8]. May my life today offer more than fig leaves—may it offer the fruit of lips that give thanks to Your name.*

Have you been fruitful with your wealth? . . . your talent? . . . your time? What are you doing for Jesus now? —*Charles Haddon Spurgeon*

See maps on pages 98-99, 112.

AN INDIRECT ROUTE

EXODUS 13:17-18

The nation of Israel began their journey from Egypt to the Promised Land by promptly turning away from it. Rather than take the direct coastal route to Canaan, God directed Israel southeast toward the Red Sea. The direct route led through the land of the Philistines, and while God could have just destroyed the enemy (as He would at the Red Sea), His concern lay more with the unprepared and fearful hearts of His people (see Exod. 13:17).

God had yet to give the people His Word at Mount Sinai, and they didn't yet have the heart to obey it. God's deliverance by parting the Red Sea paved the way for Israel to meet God face to face at Sinai—and to receive the Law by which they could live in the Promised Land.

If the goal was simply a destination, God seemed a poor travel agent. A journey of three weeks would ultimately take 40 years! But God purposed to give His people something far greater than a parcel of land; He offered them a changed heart. The land, the journey to it, and even God's Word along the way came as but the means by which they would learn to know and trust Him.

In our lives, we must realize that God's goal for us—the best He could possibly give us—isn't found in simply taking us from here to there. It isn't even found in a new biblical insight. These come as but the means of His goal—to know Him. So the Lord often leads us according to the needs of our heart, not always according to its desires.

Father, You see the fear buried in my heart that the quick and easy way would bring out. So take me directly to Your Word—take me to Your presence—that there I may find more than my own impatient leanings would ever offer.

Spiritual growth consists most in the growth of the root, which is out of sight. —*Matthew Henry*

See maps on pages 28-29, 42-43, 56-57.

GOD WITH US?

EXODUS 17:1-7

Barely a month out of Egypt, God's people grumbled to Moses at Rephidim, figuring Moses had led them out of slavery to kill them all with thirst. So Moses renamed the spot *Meribah*, meaning "quarreling," and *Massah*, meaning "testing"—for there they tested the Lord. To answer the Israelites' grumblings, the Lord told Moses, "I will stand before you there on the rock at Horeb, and you shall strike the rock, and water will come out of it, that the people may drink" (Exod. 17:6). In spite of the Israelites' repeated whining, God repeatedly provided for them fresh water, fresh meat, manna from heaven and even a day to rest.

We read these accounts of the Hebrews' complaints and shake our heads at their lack of faith. Why would they suppose God redeemed them from Egypt just to let them die in the wilderness? And yet how many times do we waffle between faith and fear in the course of one day—much less a month?

The question from the Hebrews' parched tongues often sums up our own expectations: "Is the LORD among us, or not?" (v. 7). But put this assumption to logic: Must God really follow our rules? Do our circumstances prove God's faithfulness, or do circumstances occur to prove our own (see Phil. 4:11-13)? We put God to the test when we get these backward.

God's presence among us doesn't always prove itself by our standards. The same Lord who gave the Israelites water from the rock also promises us, without exception, "I am with you always, even to the end of the age" (Matt. 28:20; see also 1 Cor. 10:4).

Immanuel—God With Us—my circumstances don't define the extent of my reality; You do. You have not left me as an orphan, for Your Spirit has come to dwell within me [see John 16:14-18]. What more could You do to convince me of Your presence?

Nothing ousts the sense of God's presence so thoroughly as the soul's dialogues with itself—when these [dialogues] are grumblings.
—Friedrich von Hugel

See maps on pages 28-29, 42-43.

A REFRESHING TRUTH

EXODUS 17:8-13; EPHESIANS 6:10-18

After God miraculously provided water for His people, Amalekite warriors confronted the Hebrews at a place called "refreshments," or Rephidim. On a hill above the battle, Moses held up his staff with both hands. As long as Moses lifted the staff of God, Israel prevailed against the Amalekites. But as soon as his weary arms dropped, the enemy began to win.

The action clearly revealed the means of victory in battle—a principle illustrated by the name of one we see in this passage for the first time in Scripture: *Joshua,* "The Lord Saves." Only by absolute dependence on God can God's people rise above their enemies. At Rephidim, through the means of water and war, God taught Israel a truth they would need in the Promised Land: He alone gives provision and protection.

This principle remains just as real in our spiritual life. Our greatest enemy is not a nation, but a spiritual being, Satan, who has nothing less than our complete destruction as his patient pursuit. He prowls around like a lion, looking for those who fail to keep alert (see 1 Pet. 5:8).

Because we face a spiritual enemy, the apostle Paul refreshes our minds with the lesson of Rephidim: "Be strong in the Lord and in the strength of His might" (Eph. 6:10). Because we fight a spiritual battle, we brawl with the weapons of God, such as truth, faith, Scripture and prayer. Our spiritual provision and protection come from reliance on God. When we fail to pray, to stand on Scripture, or to believe the truth, we fail to prepare for a battle that we cannot win in our own strength.

> Time and again, Holy Father, You reveal I must not live independent of You, but rather in complete dependence on You. As I close my eyes in prayer, help me to see the truth: The invisible world looms just as real today as the world that dominates my sight.

The devil does not sleep . . . therefore, you must never cease your preparation for battle, because on the right and on the left are enemies who never rest. —*Thomas à Kempis*

See map on pages 42-43.

68

BLESSED UNITY

PSALM 133

During his reign, King David experienced revolts—heart-wrenching family squabbles. These struggles served as a black backdrop to his declaration in Psalm 133:1: "Behold, how good and how pleasant it is for brothers to dwell together in unity!"

In the psalm, David compares unity to precious oil that anoints the head of the high priest Aaron. There is so much oil poured on the priest's head—an almost wasteful amount—that it runs down off his robes! David then compares unity to the melting snows of Mount Hermon, far in the north, which form the headwaters of the Jordan River. By having "the dew of Hermon" (v. 3) come down upon the dry mountains of Zion (Jerusalem), David described something that never occurs geographically, but the exaggeration suggests, "Imagine if it *did* actually happen!" When brothers dwell together, David said, the blessing is like a multitude of cool, refreshing streams that flow in places that desperately need it.

69

Unity is good and pleasant but also, sadly, rare and infrequent. David knew this firsthand: His aggravated son Absalom lived in Jerusalem for two years, in the same 10 acres as himself, but they never spoke a word. There's a big difference between dwelling together and dwelling together *in unity*.

Many a home has those who dwell together. Many churches have believers who worship under the same roof. But when we fail to dwell together in unity, it's like pouring gallons of olive oil on the ground or flushing streams of fresh water. The path to unity begins with personal humility and forgiveness. The results come directly from God—overflowing *blessing*.

> Lord, peace on Earth begins with peace in the home and in the Church. And peace in these places begins with me. Give me the humility to listen to others with sincerity. Help me forgive as I've been forgiven. Show me the blessing of unity so that I'll never again retreat to feeling I alone am enough.

Never pass up an opportunity to show mercy, extend grace, express gratitude, and give love away. —*Cynthia Swindoll*

See maps on pages 56-57, 70-71, 112.

Map 4
Galilee and the North

MI. 0   5   10   15

K.M. 0   5   10 15 20

Mediterranean Sea

70

Mount Carmel

Jezreel Valley

Megiddo •

Taanach •

Ibleam

Dothan •

Mount Hermon

Dan • • Caesarea Philippi

Hazor •

Bethsaida

Capernaum • Karnaim •

Mount of •
Beatitudes • Gergesa (Kursi)

Sea of Galilee

Gath-hepher
Nazareth

Hill of Moreh

Lodebar

Ein Harod Spring
• Beth-shean

Mount Gilboa

Gerasa (Jerash)
•

ON THE MOUNT OF OLIVES

MATTHEW 24:1-5

One morning in Jerusalem, I chose to have my devotions on the Mount of Olives at sunrise. Walking through the Old City's dark and narrow streets, I passed beside the Temple Mount and exited the city on its east side—much as Jesus would have done the day He left the Temple for the last time. After climbing the steep ascent of the Mount of Olives, I sat near its summit as the sun began to warm my back. Turning to Matthew's Gospel, I read about Jesus leaving the Temple, predicting its destruction, and sitting on the Mount of Olives (see Matt. 24:1-5).

Looking across the Kidron Valley at the Temple Mount—now crowned with a Muslim shrine—I thought about how Jesus' prediction proved true. Because Israel rejected Him, they ultimately lost the very objects they hoped to secure through His death—their Temple and their nation (see John 11:48). As I gazed across Jerusalem's sprawling panorama, I suddenly heard a sound that jerked my mind in another direction. Far in the distance, a rooster crowed . . . and then another . . . and another. Surrounded by a throng of cries, I immediately thought of Peter, who denied Christ, and all of the disciples who deserted Him at the bottom of the hill. Then I thought of myself.

The sights and sounds flooded my heart that morning. What I saw before me represented Israel's rejection of Christ. What I heard symbolized Peter's denial of Christ (see Luke 22:60-61). But what I felt within I couldn't relieve with closed eyes or ears. *My* sin also put Christ on the cross. That rooster crowed for *me*.

Lord Jesus, Israel rejected You, Peter denied You, Judas betrayed You, the rest deserted You—and I threw my lot in with them all. You didn't just die for a guy who needed a little help to heaven. I am totally depraved and in need of Your grace. O how I worship You today for giving Your life to pay for my sin.

I will love you, O Lord, and thank you, and confess to your name, because you have forgiven me my evil and nefarious deeds.
—*Augustine of Hippo*

See map on page 112.

CHRONOLOGICAL GYMNASTICS

EXODUS 23:15; ROMANS 8:32; PHILIPPIANS 4:19

God required the Hebrews to celebrate the Passover and Feast of Unleavened Bread at the appointed time of *Abib* (see Exod. 23:15), a Hebrew word (also spelled "Aviv") that refers to the time in spring when the grain begins to ripen. The first Passover occurred on the fifteenth day of *Nisan*, which became the first month of the Jewish calendar.

Because the Jewish month goes from New Moon to New Moon, or every 29 1/2 days, the Jewish year loses 11 days according to the solar calendar each year. And because the sun determines the seasons and controls a plant's development, the Hebrews had to compensate to make the lunar month of Nisan correspond to the month in which *Abib*, or springtime, occurred each year. So, about every third year they added an additional month to make up for the difference in calendars.[2]

73

This was all done for a good reason. The Lord gave the Hebrews a plain explanation why the celebration should coincide with spring: "For [then] you came out of Egypt" (v. 15). If the nation didn't add the extra month, the lunar calendar would cause the date for the Feast of Unleavened Bread to wander through the seasons year by year. Without the additional month, the holiday would still preserve its historical value, but it would have lost its agricultural connection to the Promised Land.

These chronological gymnastics revealed a simple lesson: By keeping the union between the Exodus and the spring, the Hebrews had a consistent, tangible reminder that the same God who redeemed them also provided their sustenance each year. This principle has not changed for us (see Rom. 8:32; Phil. 4:19).

Lord, You did not spare Your own Son, but gave Him for us all. So why would You not also give us all things? I thank You for supplying my physical and spiritual needs—just as You did with Israel. Thank You for caring.

Whilst thou eatest or drinkest let not the memory of thy God that feeds thee pass from thy mind; but praise, bless, and glorify him.
—*Richard Rolle*

See maps on pages 28-29, 56-57.

WISDOM IN OUR WAY

PROVERBS 8:1-21; 9:13-18

In stark contrast to the warning in Proverbs 5–7 on how a man's lust for a woman produces death, Proverbs 8 points the naïve to that which desirable things can't compare: wisdom. In this chapter, Solomon personifies wisdom as a woman calling out to men—a voice that leads them to life, not death. Rather than chase her audience, she positions herself at strategic settings they will undoubtedly pass: on hilltops, at crossroads, at the city gates and upon the thresholds of doors. She chooses as her podium places where men cannot miss her message (see Prov. 8:1-3).

Wisdom still stands in these places today, at places perhaps unexpected, and at the crossroads of vulnerability in our lives. Walking near, we hear what we need before we walk on. If we have the courage to listen—to really listen—wisdom can alter both our route and resolution. Perhaps we turn around. Maybe we continue on the right path but are now challenged to persevere. While her voice may have grown faint with time and distance, her wisdom still compels us to consider our paths. Like a *mezuzah* on the doorposts of Jewish homes today, wisdom serves as a daily reminder to live according to God's Word.

But wisdom is not the only voice positioned at these strategic settings. The "woman of folly" also horns her way in to our attention and, if we're not careful, to our affections. Her siren's song of compromise has the unspoken goal of our ruin (see 9:13-18).

So God has put wisdom in our way—an unavoidable voice requiring us to make a choice. We have to step over wisdom, walk around her, or embrace her. God's wisdom, distilled in the pages of Scripture, invites us to yearn for her above any other lust or longing.

> *God, thank You for the people, places and passages of Scripture You have hurled in my path to shake some sense into my heart at critical junctions of my life. Give me ears to hear, I pray, as I pass through the gates today.*

The secret of counteracting our bent toward waywardness rests with *wisdom*. . . . She is calling for our attention. She doesn't want us to drift throughout the day without taking her along as our companion.
—*Charles R. Swindoll*

See map of the city gates of Jerusalem on page 112.

BETWEEN HIS GOING AND COMING

MATTHEW 25:32-40; ACTS 1:7-12

When Jesus comes again to reign on Earth, He will land on the Mount of Olives to fulfill a prophecy that He made there in His Olivet Discourse (see Matt. 24). He will judge the nations like a shepherd separates the "sheep" (believers who are alive at His coming) from the "goats" (unbelievers) in a mixed flock.

Joel wrote that the Lord will gather the nations for judgment in the Valley of Jehoshaphat (which means, "the Lord judges") or the Kidron Valley below the Mount of Olives (see Joel 3:1-2). Zechariah also notes that the Mount of Olives will be divided from east to west by a very large valley (see Zech. 14:4). Presumably, the sheep and goats will be placed on opposite sides.

Looking at the geography of the place, one realizes the uncanny coincidence that those "goats" whom Jesus will put on His left will be gathered close to the Hinnom Valley (*Gehenna* in Greek)—the place Jesus often used as a depiction of hell (see Matt. 18:9). The sheep to His right will be positioned ready to enter the eastern gate of Jerusalem— and the Temple Mount.

Maybe because the Mount of Olives would be the place of His coming, Christ also chose it as the place of His going—for from there He ascended into heaven (see Acts 1:7-12). Between these two events— His going and His coming—Jesus gave believers the task of being His witnesses to the ends of the earth. Or, to borrow from His own metaphor, of sharing the message of the sheep with the goats.

Lord Jesus, the earth-shattering geographic changes that are coming seem no less incredible than the changes You have wrought in my heart. Beyond simply bleating out a formula for salvation, grant me compassion to share with others what others shared with me.

Preach the gospel every day; if necessary, use words. —*Francis of Assisi*

See map on page 112.

The golden cross atop the Church of the Holy Sepulcher in Jerusalem marks the traditional place of Jesus' crucifixion (see Day 44).

The façade and entrance of the Church of the Holy Sepulcher. Much of the church's structure today dates from the time of the Crusaders. The possessive sects of Christendom who worship in the church can't agree on who should remove the ladder in the center of the picture. Thus, it has remained where it stands since at least 1860 (see Day 44).

LEST I FORGET GETHSEMANE

MATTHEW 26:30-46

At the base of the Mount of Olives today lies a small grotto that produced evidence of an ancient oil press, the meaning of the name "Gethsemane." Byzantine Christians believed that Jesus left His disciples at this place while He went a stone's throw away to pray in the garden. "Sit here," Jesus told them, "while I go over there and pray" (Matt. 26:36). Then, taking Peter, James and John with Him into the garden, He said to them, "Remain here and keep watch with Me" (v. 38). Going a bit farther, Jesus fell prostrate and prayed with passion.

Today, the Church of All Nations covers the traditional place where Jesus prayed to the Father and displays a beautiful mosaic of the event. Ancient olive trees still stand in the garden, but it's unlikely they ever beheld Christ in prayer, as the Romans cut down all the trees in the region during the siege on Jerusalem in A.D. 70.

Still, entering the Garden of Gethsemane, one can imagine the scenes and almost retrace Jesus' steps along the places Matthew mentioned: "'Sit here [in the grotto] while I go over there and pray' . . . 'Remain here [in the garden] and keep watch with Me' . . . He went a little beyond them [where today sits the Church of All Nations]" (vv. 36,38-39).

Standing in the garden, a stunning insight occurs when one turns around and sees the walls of Jerusalem so close behind: Jesus could easily see the soldiers coming to arrest Him! In fact, He said, "Here comes my betrayer!" (v. 46, *NIV*). He could see those who would lead Him to death approaching, but still He chose to stay in the garden out of obedience to the Father . . . and out of love for us.

Lord Jesus, no one took Your life—You gave it up willingly for me.
You chose to do the Father's will above Your own and thus became
my Savior—and my example.

It costs God nothing, so far as we know, to create nice things; but to convert rebellious wills cost Him crucifixion. —C. S. Lewis

See map on page 112.

WISDOM SEEN AND UNSEEN

PROVERBS 8:25-33

Wisdom played such an integral role in God's creation that the author of Proverbs 8 personified it as a person present *with* God. "When He established the heavens, I was there" (Prov. 8:27).

These eloquent verses simply mean God created the world with wisdom. We only need to look to see it: The majesty of a mountain, the depths of the ocean and the limits of our atmosphere all point us heavenward. The creation points to the Creator and, specifically, to His wisdom.

God used this argument centuries earlier to convince a miserable Job of a wisdom that surpassed all human understanding—and one that justified, amazingly, all human suffering (see Job 38:1-38; 40:1-5). Paul would use this argument centuries later to teach that the creation we see points to the invisible attributes of God, namely "His eternal power and divine nature" (Rom. 1:20). Along with this revelation comes an obligation. This is why after holding up creation as proof of God's wisdom, Proverbs turns the implications of creation on us: "Now therefore, O sons, listen to me, for blessed are they who keep my ways" (Prov. 8:32). If we observe God's wisdom so displayed in the physical realm we can see, we should trust His wisdom in the spiritual realm we cannot see. In short, the awesome creation demands we obey the Creator.

In our limited perspective, we may find it easy to doubt God's way of running the universe (or, more specifically, directing our lives). But if we really believe that the Lord Jesus Christ remains the wisest man who ever lived, we will do whatever He says. Not because we understand, but precisely because we don't.

> *God, You made all physical matter from nothing—from each speck of dust, to the enormity of Everest, to the stars I can't see in the far reaches of the universe. A God as wise and awesome as You I could never come to know unless You revealed Yourself to me in Scripture. Thank You for such special revelation.*

Too much of our time is spent trying to chart God on a grid and too little is spent allowing our hearts to feel awe. By reducing Christian spirituality to formula, we deprive our hearts of wonder. —*Donald Miller*

See images of God's creation on pages 62, 90, 104, 140, 141.

WHERE SORROW LEADS

MATTHEW 26:69–27:14

Today, a peaceful monastery in Jerusalem's southern valley offers no clue to the horrific atrocities that occurred near there in the days of Judah's kings. In Jesus' day, the city dump lay in this gorge. Some suggest that fires continually burned the trash, and so Jesus used the smoldering landfill as an illustration of hell's eternal flames.

One has to wonder if this is the reason Judas's desperate regret led him to this ravine known as the Hinnom Valley. For here, according to tradition, the guilt-ridden betrayer of Christ hung himself and then fell headlong, spilling his innards. Hence, the residents later named the place "Hakeldama," or "Field of Blood" (see Acts 1:18-19). On that same day, Peter committed a sin just as wrong as Judas did, and yet Peter's regret just resulted in a good cry (and a changed life). What made the difference?

Like these two disciples, as we come face to face with the raw truth of our carnal hearts, our guilt will lead us in one of two directions. As Paul wrote, "For the sorrow that is according to the will of God produces a repentance without regret, leading to salvation, but the sorrow of the world produces death" (2 Cor. 7:10). While Judas's sorrow led him to a needless, desperate act—bowing to sin's penalty—Peter's sorrow led him to grace . . . *to seeking sin's remedy.*

God intends the pangs of shame to lead us away from our guilt and toward His grace. For although sin leads us down into the Hinnom Valley, Jesus offers us the path back out—up to Calvary. With our sins forgiven, we then have no reason to feel shame but every reason to embrace the new life Jesus offers.

Lord of grace, the only difference between these disciples—in and of themselves—was that You opened Peter's eyes to grace one day. I confess that my life, rife with sin and shame, would dangle at the end of a rope and then fall headlong into hell apart from Your gracious love. It will take me all of eternity to express my gratitude.

How sweet the name of Jesus sounds in a believer's ear: It soothes his sorrow, heals his wounds, and drives away his fears. —*John Newton*

See map on page 112.

FREE TO OBEY

EXODUS 34:10-14

Just as God miraculously delivered Israel from the Egyptians in a land of bondage, so God would deliver His people from the Canaanites in the land of promise. But with the winning also came a warning: "Watch yourself that you make no covenant with the inhabitants of the land into which you are going, or it will become a snare in your midst" (Exod. 34:12). God had delivered the Hebrews from slavery, but the responsibility to remain faithful, in spite of God's persuasion, lay squarely with God's people.

God's timeless warning to watch ourselves speaks not only to the temptations this world offers but also reminds us of our vulnerability to them (see 2 Cor. 6:14). The same weaknesses that bound us to sin in the old life we bring with us into the new. God delivered us from sin's slavery in order to obey Him, not so that we would submit ourselves again to sin's shackles (see Gal. 5:1).

We can all look back and say, after recoiling from the results of foolish decisions, "If I had only known, I never would have done it." God warns us for this reason, so we'll know the path of wisdom. But if we refuse to walk God's path, even as believers, experience will teach us what we refuse to learn through instruction.

Thankfully, Jesus' death on the cross has freed us from sin's power to control us (see Rom. 6:14). The bad news is that when we sin, we have no excuse. God set us free so that we may be free indeed to obey Him in a land of snares.

> O God, I sit amazed that You would so desire my devotion as to say You are jealous when I look elsewhere. Thank You that Your Word builds a wall around my wandering heart to warn me of my inclinations to sin and of the world's inclination to tempt me. Your jealousy both warns me and woos me to worship only You. Receive my worship, Lord, this moment.

Obedience is the road to freedom, humility the road to pleasure, unity the road to personality. —C. S. Lewis

See maps on pages 28-29, 56-57.

THE PLACE OF THE SKULL

MARK 15:22-47

The earliest and strongest Christian tradition places the location of Jesus' crucifixion, burial and resurrection to a site in Jerusalem that today has no inkling of its original appearance. The Aramaic name of this rocky outcropping, Golgotha (*calvaria* in Latin), reflects death in its translation: "The Place of the Skull."

The name of the church built over the site evokes images just as eerie—The Church of the Holy Sepulcher ("sepulcher" means a crypt or tomb). After entering the building today, those accustomed to Western worship may indeed feel aghast: gold drips from icons, chanting fills the spaces, and incense rises between cold stone walls. Six sects of Christendom display jealous rivalries over the goings-on within.

But if we look past the traditionalism to the tradition of history, we find an unbroken connection to the central event of all time. The Jerusalem Christian community held worship services at this site until A.D. 66,[3] and during the fourth century, Constantine built a church on the site to memorialize the place of Christ's resurrection.

Since that time, the church has been built, rebuilt and expanded (much of what we see today stems from the Crusader period), and different religions, races and sects have obscured much of the original site. Yet Christian tradition declares that it is at this place that Christ most likely died and rose again. Ironically, in the very place where the religiously jealous fight over rights, rules, and whose faith is in charge, the need for Christ's death still remains clear: *Religion couldn't get us to God—we needed our Savior*. The central shrine of Christendom thus demonstrates the need for the place it hallows.

> *Father, I pray that my life would be a door of authenticity for others to come to You, not a barrier they must evade. Help me never to obscure the evidence of Christ's death and resurrection behind walls of religious hypocrisy.*

This [tomb] certain impious and godless persons had thought to remove entirely from the eyes of men, supposing in their folly that thus they should be able effectually to obscure the truth. —*Eusebius, Bishop of Caesarea*

See map on page 112.

82

SIGHT AND INSIGHT

MARK 8:17-33

"Having eyes, do you not see?" (Mark 8:18). Jesus' question to His disciples revealed the purpose for the miracle that followed: When Jesus gave *sight* in stages to the blind man in Bethsaida, the miracle represented the *insight* He was giving to the disciples in stages. The disciples had a correct understanding of Jesus, but their vision was a bit blurry.

So Jesus began to clear the fog by taking them north to Caesarea Philippi. There, in an area rife with idols, Jesus asked His disciples what the people thought of Him. The disciples replied that the people saw Jesus as a prophet of old. Jesus then asked how *they* saw Him. Speaking for the group, Peter's response, "You are the Christ" (v. 29), indicated that while he understood Jesus' *person,* he did not comprehend Jesus' *purpose*: to die and rise again. Although the disciples had a correct view of Christ, they still saw Him through the fog of their own expectations.

83

Appalled by the notion that the Messiah would die, Peter rebuked the Son of God. Imagine! Jesus reproved Peter in return, but then also revealed that the reason Peter failed to fully know Him stemmed from Peter's refusal to place God's interests above his own.

Just as the blind man saw in stages and the disciples understood in stages, so you and I have much to learn about the One whom we worship. A God who is infinite reveals Himself to the finite bit by bit. Even if we know Jesus well, He still has much to reveal to us about Himself. Christ did not come to follow us and our interests but that we should follow Him and His interests.

All-knowing God whom I long to know, while the world sees Jesus as a mere man, I see Him as Peter did—from the mere perspective of man. As You reveal Yourself to me more clearly, help me embrace the cross You call me to bear—the cross that spans the chasm between who You are and who I want You to be.

You may know God, but not [fully] comprehend Him. —*Richard Baxter*

See map on pages 70-71.

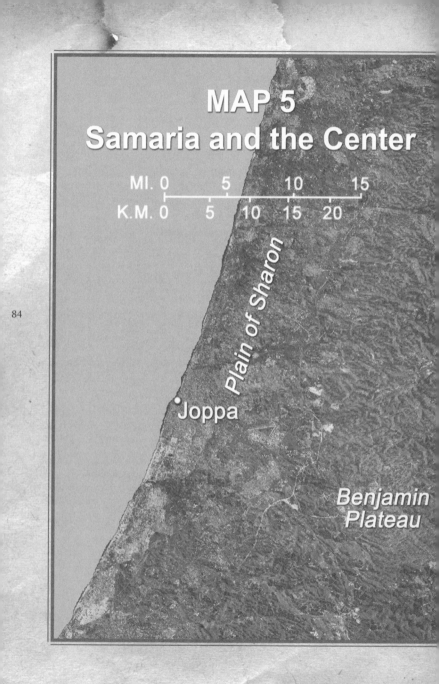

MAP 5
Samaria and the Center

MI. 0   5   10   15
K.M. 0   5   10   15   20

Plain of Sharon

•Joppa

*Benjamin
Plateau*

84

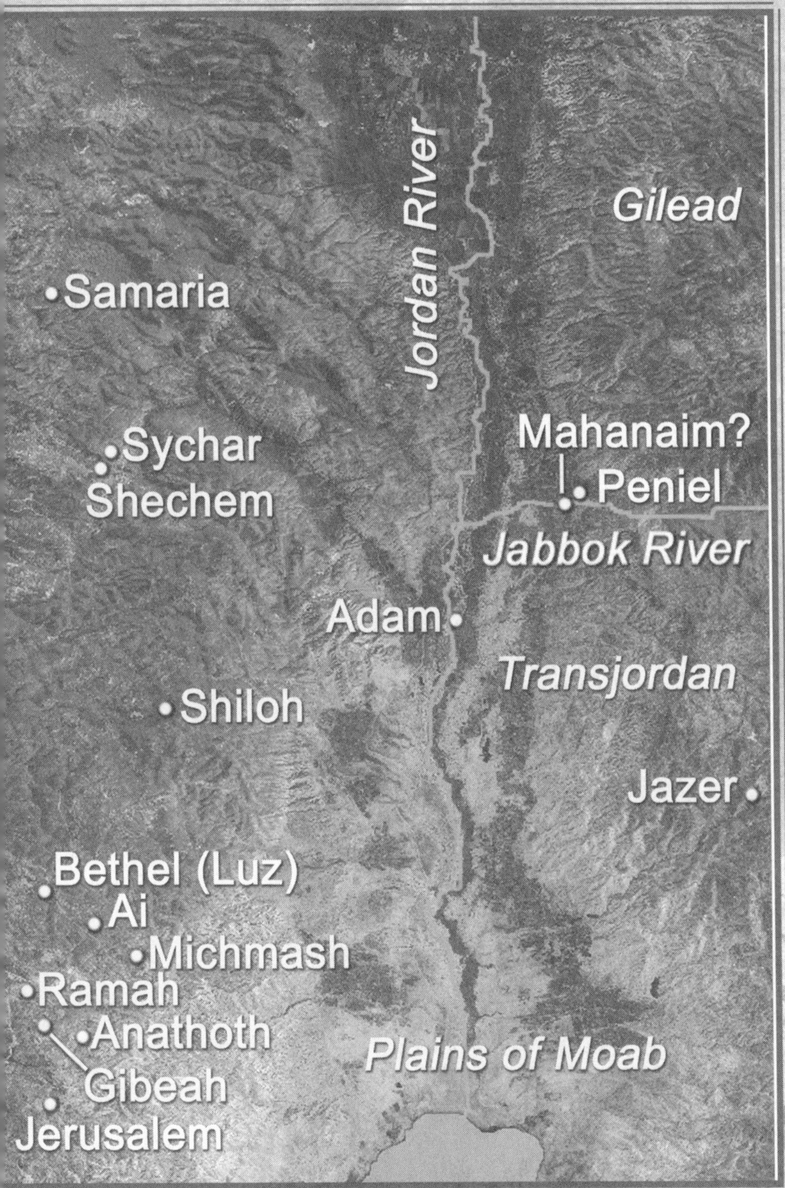
Gilead
Jordan River
Samaria
Sychar
Shechem
Mahanaim?
Peniel
Jabbok River
Adam
Transjordan
Shiloh
Jazer
Bethel (Luz)
Ai
Michmash
Ramah
Anathoth
Gibeah
Jerusalem
Plains of Moab

BOUND FOR THE PROMISED LAND

JEREMIAH 31:1-40

Possession of the physical land of Israel remains the major point of conflict today in the Middle East. Yet while the Bible allowed for foreigners to live in the land, God had always promised the land itself to the Hebrews.

As Abraham left one land to go to the place God had selected for him, God promised him land, descendants and blessing (see Gen. 12:1-3). The Mosaic Covenant promised either rain or drought on the land, depending on the obedience of Israel to the Law (see Deut. 28:12,24). The Davidic Covenant gave a promise directly tied to the land, for God told David that the Messiah would one day rule on David's throne (see 2 Sam. 7:10-16). Because God's promises to Israel always related to the land, His ultimate judgment against His people came when He removed them from it: the first time because they refused to follow Him (see Prov. 10:29-30), the second time because they rejected their Messiah. But God's New Covenant with Israel offered a changed heart through the death and resurrection of Jesus Christ (see Luke 22:20). The hope of this ultimate restoration promises a final, permanent return to the land (see Jer. 31:31-34).

While the modern immigration of Jews to Israel—and its statehood in 1948—gives us reason to hope in the ultimate fulfillment of the New Covenant, it's just as easy for God to remove them from the land as to put them there. (Remember, He's already done it twice.) God's goal through all His covenants was to have a relationship with His people, not just to make them promises and to give them gifts. All the excitement about the land itself stands feeble without the Jews' spiritual return to God—through Christ.

> God of Israel, my heart longs to see the Jewish people saved [see Rom. 10:1]. What a privilege the Jews have given me through Jesus. What a privilege they also will enjoy in Him one day.

Next to Christ's coming in the clouds, the most joyful [event will be as] the Jews and Christ fall upon one another's necks and kiss each other.
—*Samuel Rutherford*

See map on pages 56-57.

LAND OF MILK, HONEY AND GIANTS

NUMBERS 13:17-33

The nation of Israel possessed almost all they needed to enter the Promised Land. They had the Law revealed at Mt. Sinai, a strong leader in Moses and, best of all, the presence of God among them. But before God promoted Israel, they needed a final exam.

At Kadesh Barnea, south of Canaan, Moses dispatched 12 spies throughout the land to bring back a report. When they returned, the men described the region just as God had promised they would find it: "a land flowing with milk and honey" (Exod. 3:17; see also Num. 13:27). The phrase meant that the land contained an abundance of wild vegetation (for herds) and flowers (for bees)—an appealing description to a nation of shepherds. But the land also revealed an intimidating problem, for the spies saw "men of great size" there (Num. 13:32). The majority of the spies focused on their weakness and not on God's strength. The nation possessed all they needed to enter the land—except the faith to advance.

Put yourself in their sandals. What if you could send scouts into your future, have them look around, and bring back a report of what awaits you? Would you be too fearful to face the inevitable? Like the spies, would you claim that it was impossible to proceed?

In a way, these spies have revealed our future as well. The plans God has for His children lie along a path of blessing and hardship. The land of milk and honey has giants. The only way to move ahead in God's will comes by faith in God's power above our own (see Hab. 2:4). So let us trust the Almighty, who never lets one promise fall to the ground, and face the future with faith.

Almighty God, I know tomorrow holds nothing that frightens You and that You can strengthen me to do what You command. Give me the eyes of Caleb, who saw not the size of the obstacles, but the size of his God [see Num. 13:30].

Our help is in the name of the Lord, but our fears are in the name of man. . . . We fear men so much, because we fear God so little.
—*William Greenhill*

See maps on pages 42-43, 56-57.

NOT AHEAD OR BEHIND

NUMBERS 14

Which seems worse: refusing to follow God though He promises success, or stubbornly pressing forward without Him? Israel swung on both extremes of this pendulum in the course of one day.

At Kadesh Barnea, the 12 spies' mixed report of the land shot so much fear throughout the nation that they plotted among themselves to choose a leader and head back to Egypt (see Num. 14:4). They refused to follow God on a mission He had guaranteed to succeed, preferring bondage to a future requiring faith. Because of their rebellion, God announced that they would have a 40-year hiatus in the wilderness before their children would enter the land (see v. 33).

Amazingly, the people then announced a change of heart and a resolve to enter! But Moses warned them, "Do not go up [into the land], or you will be struck down before your enemies, for the LORD is not among you" (v. 42). Before, the Israelites had refused to follow God, but now they refused to wait on Him.

Moses' warning proved true: As they ascended the hill country—without God—they received the whipping they initially feared. The author of Hebrews later concluded, "So we see that they were not able to enter because of unbelief" (3:19). They failed to grasp that the land was not theirs for the taking but God's for the giving—in response to faith.

We can learn from the example of Israel that God's will always includes God's presence, and we will not have one without the other. A life that glorifies God comes when we walk beside Him in faith—not ahead or behind.

> *My God, You are my inheritance and not simply the means by which I get what I want. My goal is not a place to go, but to journey beside You wherever I go. What good would I have anywhere without You? The real blessing is simply Your presence.*

I'll go with Him, with Him all the way. —*E. W. Blandy*

See maps on pages 28-29, 42-43, 56-57, 98-99.

THE LONG WAY

NUMBERS 21:1-5

When the King of Arad captured some of the Hebrews on their way to the Promised Land, God's people cried out to the Lord and received a great victory. But instead of entering Canaan from the south where the people now stood, God led them east around Edom. As a result, the people "became impatient because of the journey" (Num. 21:4). Why take the long way around? The extra miles seemed pointless.

But as the passage unfolds, we read how God gave Israel victories all up and down the King's Highway so that they ultimately gained control of the majority of Transjordan. This allowed them to prepare to cross over the Jordan River into the Promised Land at a location far more strategic than from the south. The long way ended up the best way after all.

Often, it seems as if God needlessly extends our journey. For years we pray for a loved one's health, a friend's salvation, or for a missionary to receive funds. We plug away endlessly at a miserable job with no promotion. The long way seems the wrong way and, like the Hebrews, we become impatient because of the journey.

Yet when we look back in hindsight, we actually come to appreciate how God used the journey—and all the victories and failures along the way—to prepare us for something we felt ready for much earlier. While we strain to see over the next horizon, God sees the map from above—and so knows the best way to proceed.

Lord God, time and again Your mysterious leading proves wiser than my impatient pleas for progress. Would You not receive more glory from my life if I trusted You along the path of the unknown than if I saw Your purposes from the start? I follow because of who You are and not because I understand.

So many of us are impatient with our faith. The journey we are invited to undertake is a long haul and delivers its benefits in the longer term. We have got to learn the hardest of all lessons—that we need to be patient.
—*Alister McGrath*

See maps on pages 56-57, 84-85, 98-99.

The beautiful falls at Caesarea Philippi in northern Israel help form the head-waters of the Jordan River. In ancient times, the fertile area attracted many idol worshipers and provided an intriguing backdrop for Jesus' question, "Who do people say that I am?" in Mark 8:27 (see Day 45).

The city of Caesarea Philippi had a spring that flowed from a large cave. Here, the god Pan was worshiped as sacrifices were thrown into the cave. Niches to the right of the cave held statues of Pan.

MAKING ROUGH PLACES SMOOTH

LUKE 3:3-6

All four Gospels indicate John the Baptist specifically fulfilled Isaiah's prophecy of a voice crying in the wilderness that prepared the way for the Messiah (see Isa. 40:3). The wilderness of Judea today sits virtually unchanged since the time of John. Deep valleys, high hills and rough, rocky paths set apart this barren wasteland where John preached the words, "Make ready the way of the Lord, make His paths straight" (Luke 3:4).

In ancient times, when a king would visit a foreign land, he would send workers ahead to smooth a road so that the he could come unhindered. In preparing the pathway for the King of kings, John pointed to the rough land around him and compared it to the hard hearts he saw.

John used the physical geography in his message to communicate the need for spiritual change: "Every ravine will be filled, and every mountain and hill will be brought low; the crooked will become straight, and the rough roads smooth" (Luke 3:5). The simple command that characterized John's message, "repent," literally means a change of mind that should produce a change of action.

What geographic illustration would John use to describe our hearts today? Do we seem like rocky crags or soft pathways? Do we demonstrate a barren wilderness or a peaceful pool? What in our lives would Christ have to walk around if He came to us right now?

How many hurdles I see between us, Lord. My weak ravines need filling; my proud peaks need leveling. So many rocks need to be removed to make my repentance real. Help me make these rough places a smooth path on which You can walk unhindered. O what a gracious Lord You are to make it Your goal to soften a hard heart like mine!

Would not your behavior be very different from what is now is, if you every day lived and acted without any dependence on seeing one day more? —*Jonathan Edwards*

See map on pages 98-99.

FILL MY CUP, LORD

PSALM 63; LUKE 4:1-4

The superscription of Psalm 63 notes how David prayed these verses in the wilderness of Judah, either while fleeing from Saul or, later, from his son Absalom. The "dry and weary land" that David described in verse 1 also described his own weariness, and the lack of water around him served to surface an even deeper thirst: "My soul thirsts for you." At the height of his emotional and physical distress, David sought refuge in his spiritual life. He yearned for God.

A thousand years later, as He was being tempted in this very same wilderness, a hungry Jesus quoted Scripture to Satan, reminding him that people more than bread for their life—they need God's Word (see Luke 4:4). During great temptation and physical distress, Jesus turned to the Word of God for strength.

The One who set eternity in our hearts created in us a hunger that space and time cannot satisfy. We eat, but we hunger again. We drink, but we thirst once more. But Jesus promises that whoever drinks of the water He gives will never thirst again (see John 4:14). Physical fulfillment offers only brief relief. Deep beneath the surface, we all suffer a craving that only God can satisfy. He has placed this provision in the words of Scripture.

As with David and Jesus, even in our physical struggles and suffering God still expects us to walk with Him, and He holds us accountable to do so. He calls us to love Him above physical relief . . . not just for it.

93

> *Lord, this world offers so many solutions to my hunger, but in the end they only deepen the pangs. The gnawing within my soul finds rest only within Your presence and within the pages of Scripture. So with David I declare, "You satisfy me more than the richest of foods" [Ps. 63:5, NLT].*

It is just no good asking God to make us happy in our own way without bothering about religion. God cannot give us a happiness and peace apart from himself, because it is not there. There is no such thing.
—C. S. Lewis

See map on pages 98-99.

SETTLING ON SECOND BEST

NUMBERS 32:1-5,19

The request seemed commonsense. "Let this land be given to your servants as a possession," the sons of Reuben and Gad said to Moses. "Do not take us across the Jordan" (Num. 32:5). The tribes of Reuben and Gad had huge herds, and the land of Gilead and Jazer had lush pastures. So they settled east of the Jordan River.

Yet this settling of the tribes of Reuben and Gad (and half of Manasseh) seemed more of a concession by God than His original intent. Rather than wait on the Lord and receive the best of what He had planned for them on the west side of the river, they settled for what they saw at the time. History bears the constant struggle these tribes would endure because they chose this land.

How often have we run ahead of the Lord instead of waiting for His best? A lonely believer marries an unbeliever; an eager couple makes a poor financial decision; a family joins a church for its location in spite of its doctrine. Many people fail to see God work in their lives because they fail to wait on Him to supply. The Scriptures reveal the Lord can provide anything, anywhere and at any moment—water from rocks, bread and meat from ravens, even a coin from a fish's mouth! God's promise to provide frees us to concern ourselves only with obedience to Him.

The grass will always seem greener east of the Jordan. But can God also not richly bless within His will?

Gracious Giver of all I need, help me believe that what You want to give me is far better than what I want You to give me. I only see today, but You see the implications for eternity.

Let us then look on what we have and give God thanks for it, and know that if we should have more, He would give more. —*Richard Greenham*

See maps on pages 56-57, 84-85, 98-99.

WHAT MAKES A GOOD LAND GOOD

DEUTERONOMY 8:7-20

To hear Moses' description of the Promised Land, it sounds as if it offered vast natural resources: streams, pools, springs, wheat, barley, grapevines, figs, pomegranates, olives and honey—a land where food was plentiful and lacking in nothing (see Deut. 8:9). But this good land that Moses described existed in a delicate balance of nature—and God alone tipped the scales.

Without rain, the streams, pools and springs would dry up. The fate of the crops depended on a narrow, two-month window between Passover and Pentecost (mid-April to mid-June), and the least change in climate could leave the inhabitants hungry. Because the Canaanites in the land interpreted this balance as a battle between various deities, Moses warned Israel never to forget the Lord and follow other gods, or "like the nations that the LORD makes to perish before you, so you shall perish" (Deut. 8:20).

The Hebrews would learn that God alone made the good land "good" in direct proportion to the gratitude, praise and obedience of His people. He never intended to give His people that which would cause them to forget Him. So He rigged their whole existence with an umbilical cord that stretched up to heaven.

As we bow our heads each day over warm meals and under dry roofs, we must never forget that God's gracious provision relates very little to our jobs, homes and investments. He can provide for us anywhere and at any time. All our good blessings are only good because God has made them so (see Jas. 1:17).

Lord, the very fact that You gave Israel water from a rock shows You can provide in any situation. So let me cease worrying about my needs and seek first Your kingdom and Your righteousness [see Matt. 6:31-34]. Your provision frees me to focus on You.

Prosperity is no friend to a [selective,] sanctified memory, and therefore we are cautioned, when we are full, lest we forget God.—*William Gurnall*

See map on pages 56-57.

NO RIVERS RUN THROUGH IT

DEUTERONOMY 11:10-14

When we think of the land God prepared for His people, we might imagine another Garden of Eden—a land of grassy meadows, fertile forests and rivers aplenty. But Canaan was far from paradise.

God fashioned the land to cultivate a particular *response* and *behavior* from His people: the response of faith and the behavior of faithfulness. The Lord took His people to a place where, through their dependence on Him to meet their physical needs, He would develop their spiritual lives.

Unlike Egypt, which had the Nile, and Mesopotamia, which had the Euphrates, Canaan had no major river or water source to guarantee life. Because water remained the most important variable in the land of Canaan, God used the climate to encourage Israel to trust and obey Him. The land, the Lord said, "Drinks water from the rain of heaven" (Deut. 11:11). In Hebrew, the word for "water" (*mayim*) is related to the word for "heaven" (*shamayim*). So, even in their language, God reminded His people that they drew their very existence from Him.

We find the same true in our lives today. God has not placed us in paradise but in places where He can give us something far more valuable—Himself. Through our health, finances, family and constant struggles, God shapes our spiritual lives by revealing our inability to meet our own needs. He takes us to places of dependence because He loves us. The struggle prompts us to admit we must depend on Him to receive the life that is life indeed.

Mighty God, it seems I live where either the water is scarce or it threatens to swamp me. You have placed me in a land where I must walk closely with You if I am to survive. Thank You for keeping me dependent on You.

God hath in Himself all power to defend you . . . all grace to enrich you . . . all goodness to supply you. —*Thomas Brooks*

See maps on pages 28-29, 42-43, 56-57.

ON JORDAN'S STORMY BANKS

JOSHUA 3:14–4:23

The Jordan River usually flowed a hundred feet wide at the place where Israel entered into Canaan. But because the Israelites crossed at flood stage, the river stood much wider and deeper. When the priests carrying the Ark of the Covenant stepped into the Jordan, the water ceased its flow 16 miles upstream at Adam (present day Damieh). This left a stretch of dry land some 20 miles wide for the nation to cross en masse, perhaps several thousand abreast.

Joshua compared the parting of the Jordan with the parting of the Red Sea (see Josh. 4:23). He linked the power of God that allowed them to enter Canaan with the power that freed them from Egypt. This was a *critical* comparison: The same grace that redeemed them from bondage saw them home.

I find it fascinating that our deliverance as Christians from the bondage to sin and our entrance into God's rest both stem from the same act of grace at the cross. The author of Hebrews compares entering Canaan with entering the rest God provides those who believe in Christ apart from works (see Heb. 4:1-10). Thumb through any hymnal and you will notice how often writers used crossing the Jordan River as a metaphor for entering heaven. Fanny Crosby captured this perfectly when she wrote, "In the cross, in the cross, be my glory ever, till my ransomed soul shall find rest beyond the river."

What Joshua made sure to point out to Israel we should also embrace: The grace that saved us way back when is the grace that leads us home.

Lord, from one end of my salvation to the other—from predestination to justification, through sanctification to glorification—Your grace has provided the passage my sinful soul could not earn.

On Jordan's stormy banks I stand, and cast a wishful eye to Canaan's fair and happy land, where my possessions lie. —*Samuel Stennett*

See maps on pages 28-29, 42-43, 56-57, 84-85.

MAP 6
Judah and the South

MI. 0　　5　　10　　15

K.M. 0　　5　10　15　20

Gezer•

Shephelah

Azekah•　　*El*
　　Socoh•　*Va*
　　　Adulla

JUDAH

SIMEON　　•Beersheba

　　　　　　Ara

NEGEV

Beer Lahai Roi

Sede Boker•

HRAIM

NJAMIN
rusalem
(Jebus)

Bethany

• Bethlehem

*Wilderness of
Judea (Judah)*

ebron

Jericho
Bethphage

Valley of Achor
•Qumran

Engedi•

Dead Sea

Sodom and Gomorrah
•

Arabah
Jordan Valley

GAD

REUBEN

• Machaerus

MOAB

EDOM

GOD'S WORD MADE EASY

JOSHUA 21:1-21

After Joshua parceled out the land of Canaan to the 12 tribes, the priestly tribe of Levi received an inheritance far different from the others. Rather than getting a portion of land on which the tribe could settle, the Levites acquired cities scattered throughout the other tribes.

Strategically placed along main roads, this distribution of the 48 Levitical cities among the 12 tribes meant that any Hebrew who needed the wisdom of God's Word had to travel no longer than one day to find a priest. Years earlier, Moses had blessed each tribe, praying specifically for the Levites: "Now let them teach your regulations to Jacob; let them give your instructions to Israel" (Deut. 33:10, *NLT*). The distribution of the Levitical cities made the ministry of God's Word more accessible to His people.

Today in America, where 9 out of 10 homes have a Bible (and usually more than one), people do not have to travel far for a word from God. The Lord has provided His Word through Bible translations, study tools, radio broadcasts and instant media. Our immediate access to truth—like Israel's proximity to its Levitical cities—reveals God's desire to keep His Word close to His people so that we may always know and obey Him.

Just as the Levites had no inheritance but the Lord, so too we hold nothing in this life as our own or as precious as serving God. Rather, we see our placement in our cities as a royal priesthood whose duty remains to "proclaim the excellencies of Him who has called you out of darkness into His marvelous light" (1 Pet. 2:9).

Father, the convenience of Your Word is both a comfort and a conviction. Help me not take You for granted today, but quicken my heart to seek, to receive and to share the words of life [see Ezra 7:10]. May my life be a light in dark places today.

I believe the Bible is the best gift God has ever given to man. . . . I have been driven many times to my knees by the overwhelming conviction that I had nowhere else to go. —*Abraham Lincoln*

See map on pages 56-57.

REDEDICATION

JOSHUA 24

This wasn't the Hebrews' first time in Shechem. God told them to go there after they entered the Promised Land and dedicate themselves to His Law—which they did (see Josh. 8:30-35). Now, after the conquest, Joshua again gathered them to Shechem, as if to say, "Remember how Abraham left his idols and came to this city? Remember how Jacob put away his idols here? Remember how you yourselves dedicated yourselves to the Lord here?"

Joshua challenged the people to choose nothing short of whole-hearted rededication "in sincerity and truth" (Josh. 24:14). He told them they could choose their parents' bad examples or their culture's examples, but that the ultimate decision of whom they would serve remained theirs alone. Centuries later, Jesus (whose name in Greek reflects the Hebrew name *Joshua*) said the same thing just outside of Shechem in Sychar. He told the immoral woman at Jacob's well that God seeks those who worship Him in "spirit and in truth" (John 4:23-24). Similarly, Joshua had said to serve God "in sincerity and truth."

When will we give up the pointless quest for heaven on Earth and believe that what this world promises it never delivers? Both Joshua and Jesus remind us of the need to choose our Lord over all false gods or idols—whether they be passions, possessions or people.

Shechem became a place of rededication for Abraham, Jacob, Israel and the Samaritan woman—a place where the old life was abandoned in favor of following a Lord who alone was God. Shechem can become that place for us as well. Choose today whom you will serve (see Josh. 24:15).

I have chosen You, Lord, but now I rededicate my whole heart to You in sincerity and truth. May this remain my decision each moment today.

Resolved: That all men should live for the glory of God. Resolved second: That whether others do or not, I will. —*Jonathan Edwards*

See map on pages 84-85.

NO COMPROMISE

JUDGES 1:27–2:3

The names may not sound like much to us—Beth-shean, Taanach, Ibleam, Megiddo and Gezer—cities whose residents Manasseh and Ephraim failed to drive away. So what? Why not let the inhabitants live in this region since they wanted it so badly? The Lord knew why. These cities dotted the busy international highway that represented the front door to Israel. Not taking control of these cities amounted to not locking one's doors at night.

The failure of the tribes to drive out the inhabitants defied God's command to resist the culture. Instead, God's people tolerated the culture . . . and then embraced it. Their compromise produced disastrous results, as the Lord had said, "Their gods will be a constant temptation to you" (Judg. 2:3, *NLT*).

It always seems easier to mingle with the culture than to oppose its influence—to find the middle ground rather than stand on our own. But God knows better, and so He commands us, "Do not be conformed to the pattern of this world"; "Flee sexual immorality"; "Do not covet." God gives specific commands to protect us from experiencing a danger we cannot discern on the outside.

We must guard the critical points of entry into our hearts: church doctrine, music, television, the Internet, movies and marketing. No doubt, obedience comes at a hard price, but not as hard as the results of compromise. As we consider our culture's embrace today, we must also consider God's words again: "They will be thorns in your sides, and their gods will be a constant temptation to you."

Compromise is never worth its price.

Thank You, Father, for knowing more of what I need than I know myself. My culture fights to stay entrenched in my heart—a heart I have given to You. Help me trust You, Father, and give no compromise to culture's pull—in doctrine, action or passion.

Some will obey partially [and] obey some commandments, [but] not others. . . . But God that spake all the words of the moral law, will have all obeyed. —*Thomas Watson*

See maps on pages 56-57, 70-71, 98-99.

A LAND WITHOUT ABSOLUTES

JUDGES 19:1-20

The Levite who traversed the backbone of the hill country of Israel traced several cities along a ridge-road called the "Way of the Patriarchs." Leaving Bethlehem, he journeyed north from the land of the tribe of Judah to the territory of Benjamin. Crossing the border, the Levite's servant pointed eastward and asked if they should stay the night in Jebus (Jerusalem).

Refusing, the Levite suggested they press on to Gibeah or even Ramah, saying, "We will not turn aside into the city of foreigners who are not of the sons of Israel" (Judg. 19:12). The irony of his statement soon surfaces, as the debauched night they spend in the Israelite city of Gibeah rivals the decadence of Sodom and Gomorrah.

Repeatedly, the book of Judges notes Israel had no king in those days (see Judg. 18:1; 19:1; 21:25), which means they had no one to impose a moral standard—and thus had none. The book ends in the town of Gibeah, from which came Saul, Israel's first king. As apples fall close to the tree, so Saul reflected his city's lack of absolutes in his reckless rule. Sadly, in the place where integrity should have shined, none existed whatsoever.

103

As God's people today, we also live in a land without absolutes, a land in which the only standard not tolerated is intolerance. In such a context, the striking distinction we should display should come from leading holy lives that reflect a holy God (see Matt. 5:16; Phil. 2:15; 1 Pet. 2:12). As we exhibit God's character, we will provide a pathway to the haven people expect from Christians—and so desperately need.

> Father, I long to exhibit Your character in my life—not to impress others with my holiness, but that I may point them to Yours. Help me live in such a way today that someone will see You more clearly.

The greatest single cause of atheism in the world today is Christians—those who acknowledge Jesus with their lips and walk out the door and deny him by their lifestyle. That is what an unbelieving world simply finds unbelievable. —*Brennan Manning*

See maps on pages 56-57, 84-85, 98-99, 103-104.

The Jordan River gets its name from the Hebrew word *yarad*, meaning, "go down, descend." The river begins at an altitude of about 300 feet at the base of Mt. Hermon and flows down to 1,200 feet below sea level at the Dead Sea (see Day 55).

This tomb with a rolling stone was discovered near Megiddo during the construction of a highway on Mount Carmel (see Travelogue).

ORDINARY DAYS

1 SAMUEL 17

The thrill of the battle between David and Goliath often overshadows the staggering transition it produced. Jonathan's earlier victory at Michmash pushed the Philistines back out of King Saul's territory. So, the Philistines' next attempt to invade Israel came through their advance up the Elah Valley below Bethlehem—David's hometown. Camped between Socoh and Azekah, the Philistines posed a major threat to Israel's security. But no one in Saul's army, including Saul, had the nerve to face the nine-foot-tall Goliath.

David came that day at his father's instruction to check on the welfare of his brothers in the army. Once he arrived, David recognized his heavenly Father's will and took the responsibility no one else would accept. Killing Goliath represented no greater feat than what David did daily as a shepherd. But God used this normal day in David's life to bring about his immense popularity with Israel, another advance along his road to becoming king.

Think back to the major points of transition in your own life. Did they not often occur with chance meetings, incidental conversations and referrals from a friend of a friend? David didn't come to the Elah Valley that day to become a national hero. But God often uses ordinary days in extraordinary ways.

We never know what events God will use even today for His glory. So we should always remain faithful to perform our usual tasks wherever we find ourselves—and let God make them great according to His pleasure and purpose (see 1 Thess. 4:11). Our task and only goal today is faithfulness.

Sovereign Lord, it's not my job to figure out what great works You have prepared for me, but it is my job to accept them. May I glorify You in the simple tasks that await me this ordinary day.

We find a multitude of providences so timed to a minute, that had they occurred just a little sooner or later, they had mattered little in comparison with what now they do. Certainly, it cannot be chance, but counsel, that so exactly works in time. —*John Flavel*

See maps on pages 84-85, 98-99.

THIS LAND IS YOUR LAND

2 CHRONICLES 14; 16

Asa stands out as one of the few godly kings of Judah. He once trusted the Lord in a battle in the Shephelah and defeated an Ethiopian who came against him with an army a million strong. But Asa's greatest test came closer to home—literally.

When the northern king Baasha fortified Ramah, which sat only five miles north of Jerusalem, he effectively blockaded all movement into Asa's land. Would Asa trust God for deliverance from this enemy as he had before? Sadly, Asa decided to take the silver and gold from the treasuries of the Temple (that he had dedicated to God!) and solicit help from the pagan king of Aram.

Why would Asa, who earlier had the faith to gain victory over a million men suddenly panic and look to his own devices for help? Because God took from Asa something he trusted in more than God—a parcel of land. Asa could not fathom what he would do without the strategic Benjamin Plateau surrounding Ramah. So he scrambled to get it back at all costs.

As with Asa, we often have no problem trusting God with things for which we already trust Him. But what do we do when God says to give Him our most precious possessions—our house, our job, our spouse, our children? We learn from Asa that God may remove what we depend on the most so that we will learn to trust in Him alone. As Hanani the seer said to Asa, "The eyes of the LORD move to and fro throughout the earth that He may strongly support those whose heart is completely His" (2 Chron. 16:9). God wants our trust, among other reasons, so that He may do marvelous things in our lives.

> Lord of all, no part of my life do I withhold from You. This land is Your land; this family, this job are all Yours. I trust You alone, for You alone are trustworthy. May Your searching eyes find me fully committed today!

Faith, though it hath sometimes a trembling hand, it must not have a withered hand, but must stretch. —*Thomas Watson*

See maps on pages 28-29, 84-85, 98-99, 112.

REST ASSURED

PSALM 125

I will never forget one evening during my first few days in Jerusalem. Walking back to the hotel at sunset, my eyes caught a final glimpse of the sun as it sank over the ridge west of the city. I stopped to watch, and the words hit me unexpectedly: "As the mountains surround Jerusalem, so the LORD surrounds His people from this time forth and forever" (Ps. 125:2). I had learned the psalm years before, but witnessing this image all around me secured the truth of the text as nothing else could. *Mountains do surround Jerusalem . . . the Lord does surround His people.*

Abraham saw these same mountains some four millennia ago. David lived in the midst of these slopes. The Lord Jesus died and rose again among these hills—the very reason, ultimately, the psalm can offer a believer such assurance before God.

Several times a year, Hebrew pilgrims would ascend these same mountains, singing the Psalms of Ascents. And so, dozens of times during their lifetime, these believers would travel to the hills that repeatedly illustrated their own assurance and security before God. "Those who trust in the LORD are as Mount Zion," they would sing, "which cannot be moved but abides forever" (v. 1).

Some songs are worth repeating. Assurance remains one of those refrains.

My Creator, You made those mountains to stand through countless wars, storms and the seasons of the saints who walked upon them. The hills haven't moved. Thank You for a salvation so secure and for an illustration that I can come to again and again for assurance.

Assurance will assist us in all duties; it will arm us against all temptations; it will answer all objections; it will sustain us in all conditions.
—*Edward Reynolds*

See map on page 112.

A PARTICULAR PERSUASION

1 KINGS 9:15; 10:1-24

By fortifying Hazor, Megiddo and Gezer—key cities spread along the international highway that ran through Israel—Solomon controlled all travel and trade to and from Egypt. (At each of these sites today, you can see the very gateways Solomon built.) But the king also used Israel's position among the nations as a position of persuasion. As 1 Kings 10:24 notes, "People from every nation came to visit him and to hear the wisdom God had given him" (*NLT*).

What we see here happening on a large scale remains true for us today. We may not have the wisdom of Solomon, but we all have unique gifts and abilities. Some of us are good with our hands, some with words, and some with comfort and care. We should use these to influence others for Christ.

God has given us our strategic place in life as a position of persuasion. Our family, job, church, neighborhood, vacations, gas station, grocery store, repairmen and even solicitors—all represent people we can persuade for Jesus Christ. Paul tells us in Ephesians that one of the reasons God converts Christians is "for good works, which God prepared beforehand so that we would walk in them" (Eph. 2:10).

If we believe in a sovereign God, all of life remains a divine appointment—every single day. When we begin to use our abilities and places of influence for Christ, people will tell us what the Queen of Sheba said to Solomon: "May the LORD your God be praised!" (1 Kings 10:9, *CSB*).

Great God, help me begin to recognize that the places in which You have put me hold the good works You have prepared for me—and for which You have created me. Then may I delight to do Your will.

I am only one. But still I am one. I cannot do everything; but still I can do something. —*Edward Everett Hale*

See maps on pages 56-57, 70-71, 98-99.

CROWNING CONVENIENCE

1 KINGS 12:26-30

The nation of Israel divided into two. Now there were two nations, two kings, two capitals—but still only one place God allowed for worship. King Jeroboam felt that his northern kingdom of Israel was being threatened by the worship of God at Jerusalem in the southern kingdom of Judah. So Jeroboam made two golden calves and said to his people, "It is too much for you to go up to Jerusalem; behold your gods, O Israel, that brought you up from the land of Egypt" (1 Kings 12:28).

Jeroboam appealed to the laziness of the human spirit and established an alternate and more convenient religious experience for his people. He set up one calf in Bethel, which sat right on the road to Jerusalem. The other calf he set up in the far north, at Dan.

When you see Dan with its lush springs, rivers and shade trees, you understand why the Hebrews traveled even "as far as Dan" (v. 30). In the way of amenities, it had everything Jerusalem lacked. It was like worshiping in Hawaii. In addition to offering substitute temples, Jeroboam made substitute priests and a substitute feast as well. Worship for Israel became self-worship at the altars of convenience and recreation.

What Jeroboam said to Israel the world and the devil also continually tell us: "It is too much for you to obey the Lord; try this instead." Sin always provides us a convenient and appealing substitute—in other words, a counterfeit. Ease must never determine our spiritual priorities. Our relationship with the living God must remain a matter of obedience before convenience.

Lord Jesus, You said if I am to follow You, I should deny myself and take up my cross daily [see Luke 9:23]. Help me make my daily pilgrimage without regard to personal ease. Help me live for You who died for me.

Idolatry is worshiping anything that ought to be used, or using anything that is meant to be worshiped. —*Augustine of Hippo*

See maps on pages 70-71, 84-85, 112.

IN THE GARDENS

ROMANS 5:14-21

Two gardens, Eden and Gethsemane, provided the stage for two choices that brought opposite results. Scripture vividly contrasts these choices: Adam's decision to sin had the potential of bringing condemnation to all, while Christ's decision to die for sin provided potential justification to all (see Rom. 5:18). Adam never would have eaten the fruit had he known the acute consequences his choice would bring to himself and to his race.

Jesus' decision in Gethsemane, however, brought immeasurable blessing for humankind. In the same way, our own choices can produce good beyond imagination. When a man named Mordecai Ham shared the good news of Jesus Christ to a young boy, he had no idea at the time the good that would result. Not many people know Ham's name, but through his simple faithfulness, God converted Billy Graham.

111

Anyone can count the seeds in an apple, but only God can count the apples in a seed. Only the Lord knows the staggering potential inside each decision we make. Like Adam in Eden, we can compromise God's Word in the here and now and live with overwhelming regret. Or, like Jesus in Gethsemane, we can take God at His Word—even when it costs us dearly—knowing the Father makes the potential worth the sacrifice.

Every day, Lord, I walk in the gardens of decision. Jesus made the hard choice of obedience in the garden for me—and for all mankind. Help me fight the good fight today and choose the long-term benefits that faithfulness offers.

I cannot continuously say no to this or no to that, unless there is something ten times more attractive to choose. —*Henri Nouwen*

See maps on pages 28-29, 112.

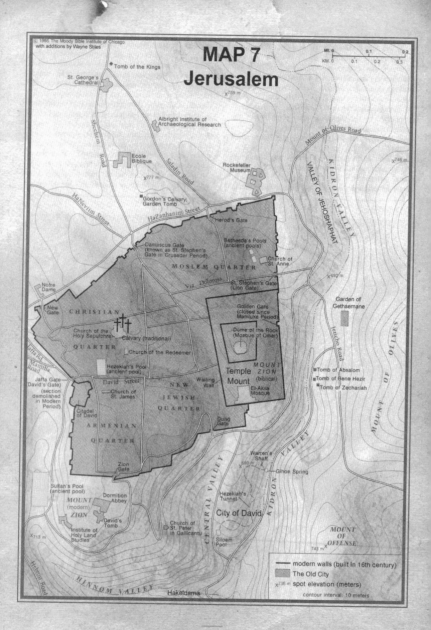

© 1985 The Moody Bible Institute of Chicago
with additions by Wayne Stiles

MAP 7
Jerusalem

MI: 0   0.1   0.2
KM: 0   0.1   0.2   0.3

✦ Tomb of the Kings

X 759 m

St. George's Cathedral

Albright Institute of Archaeological Research

Mount of Olives Road

VALLEY OF KIDRON VALLEY

X 746 m

Ecole Biblique

Shechem Road

Saladin Road

X 777 m

Rockefeller Museum

Gordon's Calvary Garden Tomb

HaNevi'im Street

HaZanhanim Street

Herod's Gate

Bethesda's Pools (ancient pools)

Damascus Gate (known as St. Stephen's Gate in Crusader Period)

MOSLEM QUARTER

Church of St. Anne

X 692 m

Notre Dame

Via Dolorosa

St. Stephen's Gate (Lion Gate)

Garden of Gethsemane

New Gate

CHRISTIAN

Golden Gate (closed since Mamluke Period)

Church of the Holy Sepulchre

Calvary (traditional)

†††

Dome of the Rock (Mosque of Omar)

QUARTER

Church of the Redeemer

Jericho Road

Jaffa Rd.—Mamilla Road

Hezekiah's Pool (ancient pool)

Waiting Wall

MOUNT ZION (biblical)

Temple Mount

Tomb of Absalom

Tomb of Bene Hezir

Tomb of Zechariah

MOUNT OF OLIVES

Jaffa Gate— David's Gate (section demolished in Modern Period)

David Street

Church of St. James

NEW

JEWISH

QUARTER

El-Aksa Mosque

Citadel of David

ARMENIAN

QUARTER

Dung Gate

Zion Gate

Warren's Shaft

X 680 m

CENTRAL VALLEY

KIDRON VALLEY

Gihon Spring

Sultan's Pool (ancient pool)

Dormition Abbey

MOUNT (modern) ZION

David's Tomb

Hezekiah's Tunnel

City of David

MOUNT OF OFFENSE

X 713 m

Institute of Holy Land Studies

Church of St. Peter in Gallicantu

Siloam Pool

743 m X

Hebron Road

HINNOM VALLEY

Hakeldama

modern walls (built in 16th century)

The Old City

X 736 m   spot elevation (meters)

contour interval: 10 meters

112

MAP 8 - Jerusalem: the Center of the World

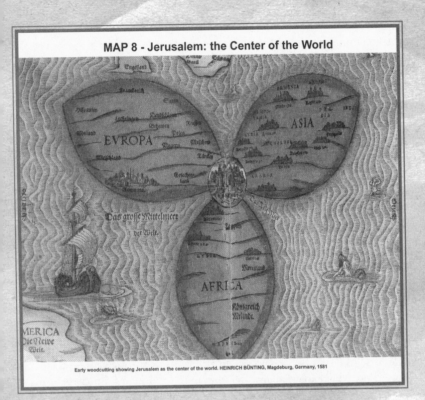

Early woodcutting showing Jerusalem as the center of the world. HEINRICH BÜNTING, Magdeburg, Germany, 1581

AND THEY CALL THE MOUNT, "MORIAH"

2 CHRONICLES 2:5-6; 3:1

The Dome of the Rock, the icon of modern Israel, sits atop a large and flat prominence in Jerusalem that Muslims call the "Noble Sanctuary," a title befitting the whole hill. For on this site, identified by Christians and Jews as the "Temple Mount," Solomon built his magnificent sanctuary some 3,000 years ago.

The chronicler states that Solomon built "the house of the LORD in Jerusalem on Mount Moriah" (2 Chron. 3:1). David had purchased the mount in his day as a place to offer sacrifice to the Lord, and another 1,000 years before that time, God had told Abraham to sacrifice his only son, Isaac, in the region of Moriah. The Lord had provided a ram to die in Isaac's place, so Abraham named the place "The LORD Will Provide" (Gen. 22:14).

A mere 500 yards west and two millennia after Abraham, another Father offered His only Son as a sacrifice for the sins of Abraham, David, Solomon and all of us. And the proverb spoken 1,000 years before Solomon came true 1,000 years after him: "In the mount of the LORD it will be provided" (v. 14).

In building the Temple for God, Solomon recognized, "Who am I, that I should build a house for Him, except to burn incense before Him?" (2 Chron. 2:6). Solomon's question gives direction for us all. Because of God's holy character and grace to us through offering His only Son, what can we really offer Him in return but absolute worship?

O God, the offering of Abraham on Mount Moriah and the offerings of David's son on the Temple Mount pale in comparison to the offering of Your Son. I can only offer You the sacrifice of praise [see Heb. 13:15].

One drop of Christ's blood is worth more than heaven and earth.
—*Martin Luther*

See map on page 112.

HERE AND THERE

ACTS 1:6-8

During Christ's entire ministry—and also after His resurrection—the apostles held as their main concern their own swift entrance into the Messiah's kingdom. Granted, the timing made sense: Now that the prophecies of the suffering of Christ were fulfilled, the promises of the kingdom of God could begin!

However, the Old Testament promised the blessings of the Kingdom to more than just the apostles and the believing Jews. "All the nations will be blessed in you," the Lord assured Abraham (Gal. 3:8). So, Christ realigned their priorities, telling them, "The Father alone has the authority to set those dates and times, and they are not for you to know" (Acts 1:7, *NLT*).

Jesus' final words to His Church came as a commission outlined by geographical parameters. The book of Acts reveals how the Holy Spirit used the Church to spread the gospel message successively: in Jerusalem (see 1:1–6:7), throughout Judea and in Samaria (see 6:8–9:31), and to the ends of the earth (see 9:32–28:31). Like ripples in a pond, the good news went out . . . but the splash began in Jerusalem.

We should begin to be His witnesses right where we live—in our Jerusalem. But our task goes beyond our own locale. Like the apostles, we can quickly crave the eternal blessings of our own interests without considering the condition of others. Could Christ be waiting for us to share with a certain person before He comes? How would we have felt if believers had asked Christ to come just prior to our conversion?

> *Lord of the nations, what an honor I enjoy as one chosen before the foundation of the earth. And what a privilege I have to take the good news to the ends of the earth. Help me balance my longing for heaven with a longing to tell others how to get there.*

Dost thou live close by them, or meet them in the streets, or labor with them . . . and say nothing to them of their souls, or the life to come?
—Richard Baxter

See maps on pages 84-85, 112.

115

NEVER BEEN TO SPAIN

ROMANS 15

The apostle Paul was about 50 years old when he penned his letter to the Roman Christians. With three missionary journeys under his belt, six books of Scripture to his credit and thousands of people impassioned for God, Paul held quite a portfolio in his hands. If Paul's career had stopped right there, no one would have protested; everyone would have stood up and applauded. Many would see age 50 as about time to start coasting and counting the years until retirement. But not Paul.

Paul continued to dream of how he could still do more for Christ. He wanted to go to Spain, the western limit of the Roman Empire. This represented a big and bold dream—audacious some might say! But Paul had a big God.

Life gets fueled on dreams. Without a purpose, we wither and die. As Christians, we have more to do than get up, work hard and come home for a few hours of television . . . only to rise and begin again. One day, we will wake up at age 65 and realize life has amounted to a stack of paychecks and a few laughs. God wants more for us than that! Christ's Great Commission blesses us with an incredible purpose: "Make disciples of all the nations" (Matt. 28:19).

So Paul planned for Spain (and also wrote seven more New Testament letters). What's your "Spain"? What's your passion? Do you have a purpose bigger than yourself? Is that purpose as big as your God?

Lord Jesus, You have blessed me with a purpose far bigger than myself. Beyond making money, may I purpose to make disciples—in my home, in my church and in my world.

There is an important dimension to hanging tough that you dare not miss. It is the thing that keeps you going. I call it a dream.
—*Charles R. Swindoll*

See map on pages 28-29.

A HIGHWAY FOR WORSHIP

ISAIAH 19:23-25

For thousands of years, an international highway stretched the full length of the land of Israel. All traffic, trade or war with Egypt had to cross the soil of this Promised Land.

In Isaiah's time, Judah considered turning to Egypt for help from the threat of Assyria. So Isaiah used this highway as an illustration of another day far in the future: "In that day there will be a highway from Egypt to Assyria" (Isa. 19:23). The travelers on this road would not have war on their minds, but worship.

In the future kingdom of God when Jesus Christ rules the earth from Israel, all nations will gather to worship Him. Isaiah shows that the very nation to which Judah wanted to run will one day turn to Judah instead and worship the Lord. Egypt will learn the Hebrew language, set up monuments to the Lord and receive His blessings: "Blessed is Egypt My people, and Assyria the work of My hands, and Israel My inheritance" (19:25).

Looking today at the Arab nations of Egypt and Iraq, this prophecy seems an absolute marvel—just as it must have seemed to the Hebrews in Isaiah's time. Yet one day, Isaiah promised, "to Me every knee will bow, every tongue will swear allegiance" (45:23), which we know will be to Jesus Christ (see Phil. 2:10). Imagine all nations traveling a highway to Israel to worship the Lord together! Then consider what a privilege we have to know the truth and to worship the Lord today.

Prince of Peace, only You can bring about the tranquility Isaiah promised. More incredible to me than the salvation of Egyptians and Assyrians is my own conversion. I worship You today—as all nations will tomorrow.

If worship is just one thing we do, everything becomes mundane. If worship is the one thing we do, everything takes on eternal significance.
—*Timothy Christenson*

See maps on pages 28-29, 56-57.

Jeroboam set up a golden calf on this high place at Dan, in northern Israel, as an alternate place of worship (see Day 64).

An aerial photo of the city of Jerusalem (see Day 66).

THE BENEFIT OF THE DOUBT

ISAIAH 35; MATTHEW 11:2-6

In preparing the way for Jesus, John the Baptist preached how the Messiah would reign forever and also die for the sins of the world. Not until after Jesus' resurrection did anyone understand how a dead Messiah could reign.

Later, while imprisoned in the castle at Machaerus just east of the Dead Sea, John felt solitude like none he ever experienced in the wilderness. No daylight, no fresh breeze, not even a locust to chew on! Just damp, dark, quiet stones. Against this forlorn backdrop, John began to nurse doubt. He even sent to ask Jesus if He was the Messiah or not.

Jesus responded by quoting from Isaiah 35:5, which spoke of the miracles of the Messiah's mercy. But the verses before and after—which John would have known as well—provided a more subtle form of encouragement to him. John was imprisoned in the very place Isaiah called "the wilderness and the desert" (v. 1). God had promised to make this barren land as fertile as Lebanon, Mount Carmel and the Plain of Sharon—the lushest parts of Israel.

John's circumstances seemed to demand doubt. But Jesus' reference to Isaiah would have reminded him that conditions would change one day. Even geography would change when Jesus' kingdom had come.

If responded to correctly, doubt can provide us a catalyst for a stronger faith. Jesus reassured John by taking him to the Word. And there we also will find the solace we need when bleak conditions challenge us to doubt. "With this news," Isaiah said, "strengthen those who have tired hands, and encourage those who have weak knees" (Isa. 35:3, *NLT*).

God, when conditions seem to imprison me in a wilderness of doubt, may Your precious promises be my refuge. May I hide in the text of Your Word.

If you would be a real seeker after truth, it is necessary that at least once in your life you doubt, as far as possible, all things. —*René Descartes*

See maps on pages 28-29, 70-71, 84-85, 98-99.

THE WORD OF OUR GOD STANDS

ISAIAH 40:1-8

Today in Jerusalem you can visit the Shrine of the Book, a museum honoring the Dead Sea Scrolls. The scrolls, which laid undisturbed for two millennia, contain our earliest copies of Old Testament books, including a complete copy of the text of Isaiah.

Prior to the scrolls' discovery at Qumran in 1947, critics had claimed the book of Isaiah had two authors, one who wrote the first 39 chapters, and another who finished it off. This claim stemmed from the fact that the two sections had different themes: the first of judgment, the second of comfort. The latter section of the book also included fulfilled prophecies so accurate that critical scholars claimed the text must have been written after the fact.

The discovery of the Dead Sea Scrolls dispelled this theory. Today, behind a large circle of glass, the museum displays a facsimile of the entire Isaiah scroll. A glance at the text reveals no break between chapters 39 and 40. In fact, chapter 40 begins at the bottom of a column—clearly showing the unity of Isaiah. Standing there in the Shrine of the Book, I noticed that prior to the beginning of chapter 40, the scribe made several errors—for instance, omitting an entire line he had to go back and insert! If the scribe hadn't made that error, chapter 40 would have come at the start of a new column, giving the possible illusion it stands separate from the previous chapters. But the mistake kept the sections unified . . . just as Isaiah wrote them.

In the wilderness of Judea where the scrolls were discovered, the grass lives a very short time. Isaiah used this fact to illustrate what the discovery of the Dead Sea Scrolls has proven: "The grass withers, the flower fades, but the word of our God stands forever" (Isa. 40:8).

Lord, You used—among many things—that scribe to verify Your Word. I praise You for defending the integrity of the Bible. I worship You for using imperfect people, like me, to pass along its truths.

The evidence of God's existence and His gift is more than compelling, but those who insist that they have no need of Him or it will always find ways to discount the offer. —*Blaise Pascal*

See map on pages 98-99.

121

OUTGROWING GOD

JEREMIAH 1:1; 2:1-13

Standing in his hometown of Anathoth on a wet, wintry day, Jeremiah could look east and see grain fields lush with life. But just beyond those fields stretched the bleak and barren Judean wilderness—a land not sown with seed.

The Lord used a similar image when He told the Israelites how they had started out as a devoted people, "following after Me in the wilderness, through a land not sown" (Jer. 2:2), but then had turned from His ways. As a young nation, Israel had left the lush Nile delta to follow God through the desert to a new land. But once in Canaan, where rain literally meant life or death, the Hebrews abandoned God and followed the Canaanites' worthless idols that supposedly gave rain.

Like many villages thereabouts, Jeremiah's hometown of Anathoth had no spring of flowing "living" water. So its residents dug cisterns—deep holes with plastered walls to catch and keep rainwater. Thus God said, "They have forsaken Me, the fountain of living waters [for] broken cisterns that can hold no water" (v. 13). In other words, the Israelites had traded the best for the worst.

It sometimes feels tempting to view God as good for salvation but a little lacking for real life. But God isn't a set of jumper cables we remove as soon as we're up and running. We didn't start out to follow God only to abandon Him when we grew up. He will always be our Father. We never outgrow the relationship. Our own efforts cannot hold water—a beautiful metaphor pointing us to trust in the Lord alone for all our needs . . . even in a land not sown.

Lord of Life, how many cisterns have I dug just to watch my life leak through the cracks? How wasted are all my efforts apart from You. Help me follow You as I did at first. May I delight to do Your will today.

The soul of man bears the image of God; so nothing can satisfy it but He whose image it bears. —*Thomas Gataker*

See maps on pages 42-43, 56-57, 84-85, 98-99.

GO TO SHILOH . . . AND SEE

JEREMIAH 7:12-14

The kingdom of Judah possessed a false sense of security. The people felt that because the Jerusalem Temple remained un-touched for centuries and the outward expressions of religion remained, they stood secure in spite of their sin. But the Lord told Jeremiah to remind Judah otherwise: "Go now to My place which was in Shiloh. . . and see what I did to it" (Jer. 7:12).

The Tabernacle, which housed the Ark of the Covenant, had stood in Shiloh for 300 years. However, because the Israelites had refused to trust in God, they lost the Ark to the Philistines, who also destroyed Shiloh (see 1 Sam. 4:10-11). In going north to the ruin, the people of Jeremiah's day could see with their own eyes what happened when God's people trusted in anything but Him. We can go to Shiloh today and see the same thing, for it remains nothing but a pile of rocks.

The example proved true. Twenty years later, the Babylonians razed the Temple in which Judah had trusted. King Herod later rebuilt the Temple, the pride of all Jews, but Jesus predicted its destruction (see Luke 21:6). Today, we can see the rubble from the destruction of the Second Temple in A.D. 70 still laying on a first-century street in Jerusalem.

We place a premium on security. Retirement accounts, insurance policies and alarm systems take a significant chunk of our earnings. Prudent, yes, but do they really provide true security? If God withdrew His hand, it could all collapse in an instant.

Let us learn from Shiloh what Judah failed to learn and put our trust in the Lord above all other securities.

O sovereign Lord, how probing are Your eyes in the heart of who I really am. While calling Your name, I have sought security in many things—some good—but things nonetheless, and idols all. Take my heart, my God, even the parts I do not know to surrender.

I'm sure I have much growth yet to experience, but I've gleaned a few insights. Probably the most important truth is that my security must be in *God* rather than in anything or anyone in this world.

—Lisa Beamer

See maps on pages 56-57, 84-85, 112.

THE CENTER OF THE NATIONS

EZEKIEL 5:5-6

The land of Israel sat in an amazingly strategic position as the only intercontinental land bridge between the superpowers of the ancient world. The most important international highway of the Fertile Crescent ran the length of the land of Israel. So any nation coming to or from Egypt, or traveling from the Mediterranean to the Gulf of Aqaba, had to go through Israel. For many years, Israel remained the crossroads for international imperialism, war and trade.

Thus by design, God intended Israel, as a kingdom of priests, to take a mediatory role among the nations. When world powers traveled through the land, God's people would either influence them for the Lord or be influenced by them toward idolatry. Because of this, Israel's central position among the nations proved to be a double-edged sword. Ezekiel records how God lamented that Jerusalem's placement as "the center of the nations" had borne no obedient fruit (5:5). Instead, God's people had been swayed by the very nations God intended them to influence.

Similarly, God has placed us where we live, work and worship in order for us to influence others for His glory (see Esther 4:14). As God appointed Ezekiel a "watchman to the house of Israel" (Ezek. 3:17), so the Lord Jesus calls us to share God's Word with those He brings to us and those to whom He takes us. He calls us to make disciples of the nations rather than to become disciples of the nations.

My sovereign Lord, I cannot even imagine what opportunities Your providence has prepared for me today! Whom will I meet? Where will I go? May I miss no occasion to bring You glory among the nations—and to bring the nations to You.

We pursue the wrong priority. We want good health, a good income, a good night's rest, and a good retirement. Our priority is *We*. God's priority, however, is God. —*Max Lucado*

See maps on pages 28-29, 113.

THIS WORLD IS NOT MY HOME

1 PETER 1:1-2

Peter addressed his first letter to Christians living in the Roman provinces of Asia Minor, now modern Turkey—namely, Pontus, Galatia, Cappadocia, Asia and Bithynia (see 1 Pet. 1:1). Roman authorities cataloged these Christians as "resident aliens" and considered them second-class citizens who could work the land but not own it. They had to join the Roman army and pay taxes, but they couldn't vote or hold public office. This inferior status, brought on by the Christians' different religious beliefs, produced hostility, suspicion and contempt within the communities in which they lived.

While the world viewed these Christians as resident aliens, Peter told them that God viewed them as aliens of another sort. Far from second-class, God saw them as of great worth—chosen, sanctified and forgiven (see 1 Pet. 1:1-6). They were great in the eyes of God, but not that great in the eyes of the world. Sound familiar?

Peter described a tension we still feel today. As citizens of heaven, we live as aliens on Earth. We struggle with living among the hostility and temptations of the world as we cling to the assurance that the God who chose us loves us more than we can possibly imagine. Our peace comes from knowing that while the world sees us as strange, we are not strangers to God. Although our mailboxes have our names on them, our real home is somewhere else (see Phil. 3:20; 1 Pet. 1:1; 2:11).

So whether we live in Pontus or Portland, Galatia or Galveston, we know our brief trials on Earth cannot compare to heaven's eternal joys (see Rom. 8:18; 1 Pet. 1:13). Here alone we must fix our hope.

Lord, I dwell here as a foreigner on the earth, and I hold nothing temporal as dear to me as You. Thank You that while I am rejected by the world I am received by You. I look forward to coming home.

Let us use the world, but enjoy the Lord. —*Thomas Adams*

See map on pages 28-29.

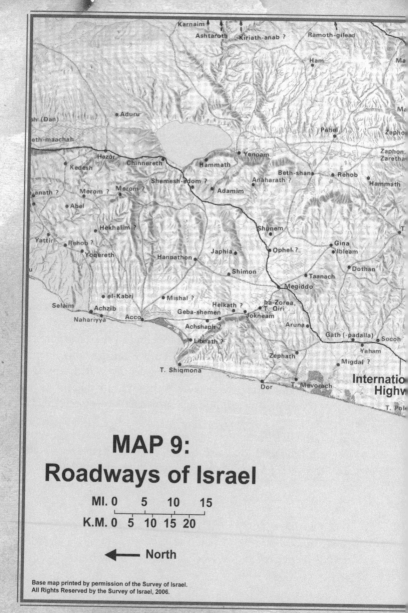

MAP 9:
Roadways of Israel

MI. 0   5   10   15

K.M. 0 5 10 15 20

← North

Transjordanian
(King's Highway)

y of the
riarchs

127

Labels on map:
Rabbath-ammon
Arom
Kh. Iskandar
Ader
Kiriathaim ?
Beth-haram
Bab edh-Dhra
Zoar
Jericho
W. el-Murabbaat Caves
Ein Samiya
Ai
Jerusalem, Salem
Bethel, Luz
Gibeon
Manahath
Bethlehem, Ephrathah
Mamre ?
Hebron, Kiriath-arba
Gedor
Beth-zur
Aijalon
Keilah
Debir
Arad
Rabbah, Rubute ?
Zorah
Beth-shemesh
Jarmuth
Eglon ?
Hormah
Aphek
Gezer
Timnah
T. Beit-Mirsim
Lod
Ono
Gibbethon
Gath
Lachish
Beer-sheba
Azor
Joppa
Muhhazi, Mahoz
H. Yavne Yam
T. Zippor
T. Nagila
T. Mor
Ashdod
Eglon
Ziklag ?
Gerar
Ashkelon
Gaza, Pa-Canaan
T. el-Farah (South)
Yurza ?
Sharuhen ? T. el-Ajjul
Deir el-Balah

DEVOTION

REVELATION 2:1-4

For more than two years, Paul lived in Ephesus and ministered to the church in that city. He later wrote the letter of Ephesians to them, and later still he wrote two letters to their pastor, Timothy. The Ephesian church received incredible instruction!

Thirty years afterward, the Holy Spirit inspired John to write yet another letter to the Ephesians within the book of Revelation. Jesus commended them highly in both their deeds and their doctrine. They labored even to the point of suffering for Christ's name. They put people to the test, preserving sound doctrine. What a church! But Jesus added, "I have this against you . . ." (Rev. 2:4). What? A complaint?

If Jesus told us today He had a complaint against us, we'd get out the checklist and start working our way down it. "Should I go on a mission trip? Should I pray more? Should I memorize the book of Romans? You just name it, Lord, and I'll do it!" But Jesus told the Ephesians, "You have left your first love" (v. 4). Gotcha.

Like the Ephesians, although we feverishly serve the Lord and remain firm in our doctrine, we can also let our devotion slip. Remember what Christ told a busy Martha about her sister, Mary, who sat at His feet? "Mary has chosen what is better" (Luke 10:42, NIV).

Our serving Christ should never replace our devotion to Him (see John 15:5). Instead, our devotion should fuel our serving. The Lord Jesus points to our first love for Him as the hub from which every other activity should flow. Let us return to that simplicity.

> Lord Jesus, when I first came to You, all I had was You—and that was all I needed. Have I grown so much in knowledge and service that my love for You has grown cold? Has the Great Commission replaced the great commandment [see Matt. 22:36-38]? Help my deeds and doctrine to be but the wake of my devotion.

The Father's pre-eminent plan is for the Son to have first place in everything. The more we adopt that as our primary goal, the more we will trust God, because that is a purpose God *will* fulfill. —*David Gregory*

See map on pages 28-29.

THE DECEIT OF PRIDE

OBADIAH

If you've ever felt the sting of a scorpion, you and I share a common awe at how something so small can produce a sting so painful. I get the same feeling from reading Obadiah, the shortest book in the Old Testament. Written to ancient Edom east of the Jordan River, Obadiah gives a stinging rebuke to the sin of pride.

The geography of Edom provided an almost impenetrable fortress. Invading armies could enter only by snaking through difficult mountain passes. This location gave the people of Edom great national security and led to some colossal arrogance on their part. "The pride of your heart has deceived you," the Lord told them, "you who live in the clefts of the rocks and make your home on the heights" (v. 3, NIV). The Edomites' misplaced pride would later become their undoing.

Edom's geography bears a resemblance to our affluence today. Our self-reliant culture crows, "Never take guff!" "Depend on no one!" "Save face at all costs!" Pride alone fuels this counsel. When we feel self-secure, we sense no need for anything or anyone else—even God. Our physical resources tempt us to reject any external influence in our lives. But as the Lord told the Edomites, such an attitude smacks of over-confidence: "The pride of your heart has deceived you."

Just as arrogance would displace the Edomites, so our pride will betray us unless we walk with God in humility (see Mic. 6:8). God never created us to live in independence from Him, but in dependence on Him. What an honor to rely on the Lord of whom alone we boast . . . and from whom alone we receive all we need.

> Lord, I confess the last stronghold in my heart is defended by pride. In this moment of honesty, I ask You to root it out. Help me learn from You who are gentle and humble of heart. In spite of the blessings poured upon me, I bow myself before You in complete dependence and adoration.

Boasting is the voice of pride in the heart of the strong. Self-pity is the voice of pride in the heart of the weak. —*John Piper*

See maps on pages 56-57, 98-99.

A LITTLE TOWN—BETHLEHEM

MICAH 5:2-5

When we listen to Christmas carols and look at Christmas cards, we often find them filled with sentimental terms such as "tidings," "goodwill," "noel," "cheer" and "Merry Christmas." Scenes on the cards typically depict a newborn with radiant beams from His holy face, oxen and donkeys bowing, with halos hovering above Jesus, Joseph and Mary.

We call the baby's bed a "manger," not a feed trough; we call the scene a "nativity," not a birth. We do all we can to take away the ignobility the Bible explicitly portrays: Christ's birth represented humility in the truest sense of the word. We've even built a church over the cave where Christ was born!

Seven hundred years before the birth of Christ, Micah prophesied that One coming from eternity would bring the Jews back to their land and rule Israel with worldwide fame in the strength of the Lord. This mighty Messiah would come from the ignoble, little town of Ruth and David: Bethlehem (see Ruth 4:11,22).

Why such unadorned humility? Because Jesus came the first time to live the life we should have lived and to die the death we should have died for our sins. The second coming of Christ is the one everyone wanted first. While Micah blended both advents into one prophesy, we understand the necessity of their separation (see Heb. 9:28). We needed a Savior before we needed a King.

The words Phillips Brooks penned in 1868 after a Christmas Eve visit to Bethlehem remain so appropriate: "In thy dark streets shineth the everlasting Light: the hopes and fears of all the years are met in thee tonight."

Lord Jesus, the only way we could ever have peace on Earth and goodwill among us was for the sin among us to be removed. I worship You for the indignity You embraced, from Your cradle to Your cross, so that we might live in glory.

If Jesus were born one thousand times in Bethlehem and not in me, then I would still be lost. —*Corrie ten Boom*

See map on pages 98-99.

YOU'RE ONLY LONELY

PSALM 139; 142:1-5

For many people, holidays and anniversaries draw up unpleasant memories. Sore spots in childhood or the loss of loved ones hit them hard during sentimental times. While many celebrate the joys of life, others suffer its loneliness.

During one of the most desperate times of David's life, the one anointed future king of Israel found himself running from two separate enemies. With the Philistines to the west and King Saul to the east, a distressed David sought refuge in the cave of Adullam (see 1 Sam. 22:1). From all human perspectives and emotions, David felt alone. Yet in prayer he confessed to God, "When my spirit was overwhelmed within me, You knew my path" (Ps. 142:3). In Hebrew, the word "You" stands emphatic, meaning only God understood David's pain. So from the depths of this cave, David cried, "You are my refuge."

David's phrases illustrate the tension between anguish of soul and dependence on God. A desperate aloneness often feels like a prison—as it did to David. Desperate thoughts and actions often follow. But when we feel overwhelmed and lonely, we should remember that the Lord alone knows us and is "intimately acquainted with all [our] ways" (Ps. 139:3). Regardless of how we feel, God's Word promises this is true.

David teaches us what we must never forget: The lonely times are the times to seek refuge in God through prayer. They're not the times to seek the world's solutions. By removing everything but Himself, God wants to teach us during these struggles what David affirmed: "You are all I really want in life" (Ps. 142:5, *NLT*).

> *O God, when I feel alone—really, really alone—I will cling to Your promises that You will never abandon me, never fail me, and never forsake me [see Deut. 31:8; Matt. 28:20; John 14:18]. Help me see loneliness as Your call for me to draw near to You.*

Oh, what peace we often forfeit; oh what needless pain we bear, all because we do not carry everything to God in prayer. —*Joseph M. Scriven*

See map on pages 98-99.

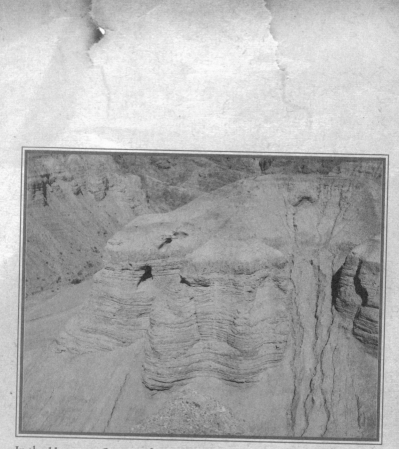

In the 11 caves at Qumran, fragments from every Old Testament book except Esther have been found. These Dead Sea Scrolls verified the trustworthiness of our copies of the Old Testament (see Day 71).

The city of Bethlehem, as seen from the area of Rachel's Tomb (see Day 78).

WHEN JESUS SHOWS UP LATE

JOHN 11

Mary and Martha of Bethany sent a message to Jesus that their brother, Lazarus, lay sick. The journey to Bethany would take Jesus two days of hard, hot, uphill travel. But instead of traveling to Bethany, Jesus stayed right where He was beyond the Jordan River. When He finally did arrive, He found that Lazarus had been dead four days. In other words, Jesus took His sweet time showing up.

From all appearances, Jesus' delay suggested lack of concern or a lack of ability (see John 11:21,32,37). Pain always tempts us to view Jesus this way. But this story reveals the exact opposite. Remarkably, Jesus delayed because He *loved* them (see vv. 5-6).

As hard as we try, we often struggle to wrap our minds around the contradiction. After all, it's hard to feel God's love when we cry out to Him, perhaps for years, but He seems to ignore us. Our pain blurs what Jesus sees clearly. For example, Jesus saw what Lazarus's death would produce—an opportunity to believe for those who would witness a miracle. He knew the sisters would grow to see that God loved them on a level deeper than simply removing pain. Here we must grow as well.

Because Jesus waited, we can know He wants to give us more than relief. Because Jesus wept, we can know He feels our pain, strengthening us with His presence along the path His sovereign will sees as best for us. He loves us enough to let us hurt so that we will gain what we could not otherwise. And He walks with us—and weeps—along the painful road that leads to death . . . but then, also to resurrection.

So often, Lord Jesus, I want You here doing my will, not there doing Yours. Thank You for lovingly ignoring my ignorant protests at Your "unreasonable" ways. Help me to look at life with Your eyes that see the end in spite of the road that takes me there.

God aims to exalt Himself by working for those who wait for Him.
—*John Piper*

See map on pages 98-99.

FROM FEAR TO FAITH

JUDGES 7

The Spring of Harod still flows from the mouth of a cave at the bottom of Mount Gilboa. Throughout the centuries, water from this spring refreshed innumerable travelers throughout the Harod Valley. And here Gideon learned to trust God.

Although God promised Gideon a great victory, the doubtful judge still requested a sign. Yet the assurance of God's promises didn't negate the circumstances that forced Gideon to trust Him. Gideon's fleece didn't cause 135,000 Midianites to disappear; he still had to trust God for deliverance.

God knew that the Hebrews, though badly outnumbered, would still boast in their victory. So God told Gideon to bring his men down to the spring and separate them on the basis of how they drank. Thinning the ranks again put Gideon in a position in which his fear would be exposed. Gideon had sought security with the fleece, and though God acquiesced to the request, the Lord immediately countered by putting Gideon in an even more precarious position. If he struggled to trust God at 4 to 1 odds, how would he react to 450 to 1?

Some situations today will seem as bleak, hopeless and pointless as Gideon's must have seemed to him at the time. Circumstances and emotions will demand that we doubt what God has clearly promised. But our confidence must remain in what God has said, not in what we see. To help us understand that, God will take us places to free us from fear and to convince us He can do what He said. We shouldn't need a sign to confirm what God has already promised, just the faith to follow Him.

Thank You, Father, for ignoring my immature pleas for relief and letting me squirm. As I face unavoidable fears, I begin to understand what escape would never have allowed: You do what You say. Circumstances change, but Your Word never will.

We trust what we know. It's difficult to trust God if we are not growing in knowing Him. If we know how deeply He loves us, trust becomes more natural, like a small child trusting a parent. — *David Gregory*

See map on pages 70-71.

FROM TROUBLE TO TRIUMPH

JOSHUA 7

Joshua must have felt terribly confused. After the thrill of victory at Jericho, the Israelites suffered the agony of defeat at Ai . . . and for no apparent reason. As it turned out, a man named Achan had taken the spoil of Jericho that God had banned and buried it under his tent (see Josh. 7:1,21).

The word "Achor" means "trouble," and so, with a slight variation of Achan's name, Joshua asked him, "Why have you *troubled* us?" (v. 25, emphasis added). After Achan's execution, the valley where he died took on the name "Valley of Achor." And years later, Israel even referred to Achan as Achar, "the troubler" (see 1 Chron. 2:7).

Just as one family's hidden sin jeopardized the whole nation's settlement in the land, so it is with us. If we harbor concealed sin in our hearts, God needn't bless our progress. We must do today what we will wish we had done when we were discovered: confess and change. The psalmist declared, "If I regard wickedness in my heart, the Lord will not hear" (Ps. 66:18).

The prophets later took this Valley of Achor—which had been linked only with sin, discipline and death—and made it a place of promise. Hosea spoke of the valley as a future door of hope and a place for joyful singing (see Hos. 2:15). Isaiah referred to the dry valley as the spot where herds will someday rest (see Isa. 65:10).

God can produce hope even in our most awful situations. We allow Him to do this by coming to terms with our willful sin. God can change our "trouble" into triumph, but first we must come clean.

Thank You, Lord Jesus, that when I acknowledge my willful, hidden sins, You purify me from all unrighteousness—even those sins buried so deep I do not know to confess [see 1 John 1:9].

One sin willingly lived in is as able to destroy a man's soul as a thousand. —*John Owen*

See maps on pages 84-85, 98-99.

AFFLICTING THE COMFORTABLE

AMOS 6:13-14

In a time of tremendous affluence, Israel went soft on God. They sought opulent furniture, the finest food, first-class entertainment, the best wine and perfumes . . . but they did not seek the Lord. So God sent a fig picker from Judah north to Israel to afflict the comfortable.

Amos spoke to those "who rejoice in Lodebar, and say, 'Have we not by our *own* strength taken Karnaim for ourselves?'" (Amos 6:13). Lodebar and Karnaim guarded the approaches to Israel's Jezreel Valley from the eastern Transjordanian highway. Israel's recent victories in those regions had given them an arrogant and false sense of security. With tongue firmly in cheek, God referred to the city of Lodebar as *Lodabar*, which means "no thing."

In other words, the Israelites rejoiced in what amounted to nothing. God would bring the Assyrians from that same direction, and they would afflict Israel "from the entrance of Hamath to the brook of the Arabah" (v. 14). From the north to the south, God would afflict the comfortable.

Take a moment of silent, brutal honesty. Where has devotion to God taken a backseat to devotion to His blessings? Maybe you have given ministry or projects more dedication than your personal time with God. Maybe keeping your home neat and nice has taken priority over kindness to those within it. Israel's blessings wooed them away from loving the God who blessed them. Are we any different?

The Lord remains committed to our relationship with Him, no matter the cost. When comfort dulls our sensitivity to God, He has little choice but to remove the obstacle.

137

Father, why do I struggle so hard to surrender the blessings I received so easily? Are they not Yours to give and take? Remind me that moths and rust destroy the things I treasure here [see Matt. 6:19]. Renew my allegiance to things eternal—to Your people, Your Word and, above all, to Yourself.

If you have anything that you prize very highly, hold it very loosely, for you may easily lose it. —*C. H. Spurgeon*

See maps on pages 28-29, 70-71.

BENJAMIN IN BETWEEN

ISAIAH 11:13-14

The sibling rivalry among the sons of Jacob passed through succeeding generations like an inherited disease. These 12 sons produced 12 tribes, and 2 of these tribes led the way in the contention. Judah, the tribe from which the Messiah would come (see Gen. 49:10) and Ephraim, a tribe from Jacob's favorite son, Joseph, continually locked horns over national control and influence. So when Israel settled in Canaan, God positioned a buffer between Judah and Ephraim—the tribe of Benjamin (see Josh. 18:5,11).

The "buffer tribe" of Benjamin possessed an enviable plateau with strategic crossroads that remained the constant desire of these dominant tribes. Israel's first king, Saul, came from Benjamin. After David became king, he relocated from his own tribe of Judah into Benjamin, choosing neutral Jerusalem as his capital. The buffer served to unify the nation by keeping peace between Judah and the northern tribes who favored Ephraim. But even in a united Israel, the rivalry never ceased.

Isaiah looked ahead to a time when Judah and Ephraim would defeat God's enemies via the routes of Benjamin (see Isa. 11:13-14)—when they would, at last, serve a cause higher than themselves—that of the kingdom of God.

Like Benjamin in between, God calls us to be peacemakers (see Matt. 5:9; Rom. 12:18; Jas. 3:14–4:1). As believers anticipating God's kingdom, we serve a higher purpose than our own interests and agendas. Rather than envy what God has given another brother or sister, we should remember the One who became humble and laid down His life for others—and then follow His example.

How common it feels, Father, to envy Ephraim and be jealous of Judah. How foreign it seems, though, to die to self for the sake of unity. Remind me today that none of us wins or loses alone. Help me to be a peacemaker in all my relationships.

If we have no peace, it is because we have forgotten that we belong to each other. —*Mother Teresa*

See maps on pages 56-57, 98-99, 112.

THE LAND RESTED

LEVITICUS 25:1-23

After settling in Canaan, God allowed His people to work the land. But every seventh year, God said, "the land shall have a sabbath rest, a sabbath to the LORD" (Lev. 25:4) and lie fallow. The Sabbatical Year allowed for the forgiveness of all debts, and any food that grew went to the poor and to the wild animals. Then every 50 years, on the year of Jubilee, the land not only rested but also returned to its ancestral owners. And all slaves walked free.

However, in 586 B.C., after God's people failed to observe the Sabbatical Year for 490 years, God exiled them for the 70 special years they failed to give the land (see 2 Chron. 36:20-21). All this was to show that the land belonged to God, not to those who lived on it (see Lev. 25:23). Although they worked the land, it was God who provided, and He made them stop working to prove it. For even when they rested, God supplied (see Ps. 127:2).

Some principles remain unchanged. Anyone who has ever lost a job or sensed true sacrifice in giving to God's work has felt the tension faith required in the Sabbatical Year. Faith involves trust and trust implies risk (from our perspective). While God is never late, He also is seldom early.

The Father longs that we understand He provides *daily* bread, not careers by which we're set for life (see Luke 11:3). God may keep us on the edge of our means, for there our need for Him is often more clearly seen.

> *God, I ask for not too little and (dare I pray?) for not too much, but only what I need to remind me I don't live by bread alone. You, alone, provide for me in daily doses. As with Israel in the wilderness before the Sabbath, so my own efforts to anxiously gather extra breed worms . . . and amount to nothing.*

O God, never [allow] us to think that we can stand by ourselves, and not need thee. —*John Donne*

See map on pages 56-57.

From atop Mount Carmel, one can see the broad expanse of the Jezreel Valley and the traditional place of Elijah's showdown with the prophets of Baal in the foreground (see Day 86).

The ancient port city of Joppa overlooks the Mediterranean Sea (see Day 87).

ALL POINT TO HIM

JOHN 1:26-34; ROMANS 8:28-39; 11:33-36

Many people recognize the association between Elijah and John the Baptist. After all, Jesus made it plain: "John himself is Elijah who was to come" (Matt. 11:14). But just as the Bible parallels Elijah and John, so it also compares those they preceded: Elisha and Jesus.

"Elisha" means "God is salvation," and "Jesus" means "the Lord is salvation." Both men performed a slew of similar miracles: They multiplied bread (see 2 Kings 4:42-44; Luke 9:12-17), healed the leprous (see 2 Kings 5:1-14; Luke 17:11-14) and defied gravity on water (see 2 Kings 6:1-7; John 6:16-21). Each raised a dead boy to life in the Jezreel Valley beside the Hill of Moreh (see 2 Kings 4:35; Luke 7:11-16).

Even more remarkable, Elijah passed his prophetic ministry to Elisha after parting the Jordan River near Jericho (see 2 Kings 2:1-14). Tradition holds that John baptized Jesus at this same site, transferring the prophetic mantle once again. But this time, instead of the Jordan parting and the spirit of Elijah coming upon Elisha, the heavens parted and the Spirit of God rested on Jesus. God used names, prophecies, miracles and even geography to underscore what John cried out: "Behold, the Lamb of God who takes away the sin of the world! . . . This is the Son of God" (John 1:29,34). Think about your own journey to Jesus. Didn't the Father use more than one friend, conversation, Scripture, preacher, or happenstance to introduce you to His Son? Doesn't He continue to use a variety of means to encourage our daily walks?

Eventually, we begin to recognize the Lord uses all things, with nothing wasted, to draw us closer to Him. Indeed, all things point to Him . . . and to our need to walk closely with Him (see Rom. 11:33-36).

O Lamb of God, I confess as John did that I am unworthy to untie Your sandal straps. Thank You for drawing me to Yourself in various ways and for confirming to me every day, in ways often astounding, that You are who Your name proclaims: "The Lord is salvation."

The way in which God heals our wound is a deeply personal process. He is a person and He insists on working personally. —*John Eldredge*

See maps on pages 56-57, 70-71, 98-99.

GOD'S WILL THE OTHER WAY

JONAH 1–4

In their attempts to discredit Jesus, the Pharisees claimed, "no prophet arises out of Galilee" (John 7:52). But the prophet Jonah came from Gath-hepher, located right beside Jesus' hometown of Nazareth! It's easy to forget about this prophet who ran from God—especially when we're doing the same.

Jonah had no desire for God to forgive the pagan Nineveh. So when the Lord told him to preach in Assyria's future capital, he took a ship from Joppa bound for Tarshish—the *opposite* direction of Nineveh! In the furious squall that followed, Jonah found himself in the belly of a great fish, confessing, "Salvation is from the LORD" (Jon. 2:9). (Of course, Jonah meant *his* salvation, not Nineveh's.)

The fish hurled Jonah onto dry land, back to the task he had run from. Again the Lord told Jonah to go to Nineveh, and this time Jonah obeyed. He preached, Nineveh repented and what Jonah feared, happened . . . God forgave them. As Jonah later sulked in the sun, watching what would happen to the city, the Lord provided a plant for shade. For the first time in the book, Jonah smiled. But then God sent a worm to eat the plant. When the heat hit Jonah's head, he became faint and begged God to take his life.

How often do we feel life isn't fair or, worse, that God has let us down because He runs the universe differently than we would? Our blessings turn into entitlements and we become more concerned with trifles such as plants than with people made in God's image. Our grumblings only betray that we're running in a direction opposite from God. In His grace, God appointed the fish, the plant, the worm and the wind . . . all to get Jonah to change. What creature comforts may God have removed from your life to reveal an inordinate preoccupation with self?

143

Thank You, Jesus, that You didn't cling to comforts when it came time to obey the Father. I know that the difficulty of submitting to You is easier than the difficulty of running from You. When obedience makes me uncomfortable today, help me choose the right direction.

God doesn't bless us just to make us happy; He blesses us to make us a blessing. —*Warren Wiersbe*

See maps on pages 28-29, 42-43, 56-57, 70-71.

A GOOD WORD FOR MARRIAGE

SONG OF SONGS 4

God began the human race with marriage. His first command, "Be fruitful and multiply" (Gen. 1:28), required the physical union the Song of Songs extols. But God clearly intended sexuality as more than a means of multiplication. He created it to crown a marriage of affirmation with pleasure.

In the Song of Songs, inspired discretion veils the couple's erotic descriptions behind the language of metaphor. Just as Wyoming's Grand Tetons veils its referent behind its French name, so Solomon refers to twin "mountains of spices" to describe the pleasantness of her anatomy (Song of Songs 8:14; see also 1:13; 4:5-6). Indeed, one such reference reveals her desire for him to be like a deer "on the mountains of Bether," literally, "mountains of separation" or "cleavage" (2:17). Because Israel had no mountains called Bether, the bride's implications are obvious.

Although the bride initially felt insecure about her looks, after Solomon's kind words, she compared herself to a rose in the Sharon Plain (see 2:1). She likened him to blossoms in Engedi, an oasis beside the Dead Sea's brackish shores (see 1:14). Likewise, he compared her head to Mount Carmel, a symbol of great elevation in Israel (see 7:5).

So many marriages today ignore the value of loving affirmation and turn instead to a critical tongue or a pointing finger. But the couple in the Song of Songs never does this. Instead, they repeatedly affirm one another in spite of their imperfections. In fact, an encouraging, godly attitude becomes the most attractive part of a person—even when physical beauty fades.

Father, for all that needs to change in my marriage, start with me. Help me apply the wisdom of Solomon and offer affirmation to my spouse— and prayers of blessing—instead of gripes, groans and eyes that roll. I give my heart to this task today, just as I vowed to do years ago.

Just think of a few affirming words—"You look beautiful today" (or your version thereof)—and say that to them. That kind of compliment might not feel natural to you at first, but if you stick with it, it can eventually feel as familiar as, "Pass the remote." —*Shaunti and Jeff Feldhahn*

See maps on pages 70-71, 84-85, 98-99.

BELIEVING IS SEEING

JOHN 20:24-31

Nineteenth-century archeologist William Ramsay began his career with the general assumption that the book of Acts contained careless, geographical errors written by someone ignorant of Asia Minor. However, after Ramsay traveled throughout Asia Minor (modern-day Turkey), he altered his position. He found the geography presented in Acts accurate in every detail—and he believed.

Many people demand evidence for truth they never intend to accept. Their problem isn't a lack of truth, but a suppression of it (see Rom. 1:18-20). While God has no problem proving Himself, He knows that proof only goes so far. For when proof removes people's excuses, they must then respond to the truth with belief.

"Unless I see," said doubting Thomas, "I will not believe" (John 20:25). Thomas wasn't the only skeptic in the bunch. Many, if not most, of Jesus' disciples struggled with uncertainty—even after the resurrection. Jesus did all He could to affirm their faith and dispel their doubts (see Matt. 28:17-20; Luke 24:38-39; Acts 1:3), but the believing part He left up to them . . . just as He does with us.

Do you ever find yourself waiting for God to prove something He has already promised? What for? (Read that again.) Hasn't God already proven Himself faithful in your life every day of every year, even during those times of deepest discouragement?

While proof may help our faith along, it never believes for us. Whether we face doubts about the geography of Acts, the provision for our groceries or the salvation of our soul, our responsibility remains the same: We must respond to the truth God has revealed by believing it.

My Lord and my God, I could save myself a lot of time (and grief) if I just believe now what You will ultimately prove. Help me receive Your words to Thomas as Your Word to me: "Blessed are they who did not see, and yet believed" [John 20:29]. I choose today to walk by faith, Lord, and not by sight.

You may press the words of Luke in a degree far beyond any other historian's, and they stand the keenest scrutiny. —*William Ramsay*

See map on pages 28-29.

THE END AND THE BEGINNING

REVELATION 22:1-5

The Bible begins with God placing the tree of life alongside the tree of the forbidden fruit. Thus, the created earth became the arena in which man could fulfill his purpose to rule under God for His glory.

The fall of man into sin cursed not only mankind but also all creation. In Malachi's final words, the Old Testament ends not far from its beginning, clutching a hope of redemption from the curse: "Look, I am sending you the prophet Elijah before the great and dreadful day of the LORD arrives. . . . Otherwise I will come and strike the land with a curse" (Mal. 4:5-6, *NLT*).

The coming of Christ provided the ultimate sanction and blessing of the earth in which He revealed the dignity of humanity by becoming a man. While on Earth, Jesus fulfilled man's original purpose of demonstrating God's glory by living an obedient life—obedient even to death on a cross. Through His atoning sacrifice, Jesus removed the curse, providing all mankind with the opportunity to "eat the fruit from the tree of life" (Rev. 22:14, *NLT*).

From the first chapter of the Bible to the last, God used the physical earth as the stage for man's spiritual life. The new heaven and earth will reproduce the same intention as the originals in that they will provide a platform for man to rule under God. By God's grace, Adam literally gets to rule again.

And so . . . let us use the ground beneath our feet for the purpose in which God created it—a place to display His glory.

O You who are the Alpha and the Omega, the First and the Last, the Beginning and the End, You will cause the end of the earth and the beginning of a new one. I long to walk in such places where I may behold Your face, rule the earth under Your authority and display Your magnificent glory forever and ever—the purposes for which You predestined me so long ago.

Heaven begins where sin ends. —*Thomas Adams*

See maps on pages 28-29, 70-71.

The secluded city of Nazareth sits surrounded by the Nazareth Ridge (see Travelogue).

The golden Dome of the Rock on the Temple Mount in Jerusalem is the icon of modern Israel (see Travelogue).

CONFESSIONS OF A CHRISTIAN PILGRIM:

A TRAVELOGUE

AT ITS HEART, A MAP IS THE DISTILLATION OF THE EXPERIENCE OF TRAVELERS—THOSE WHO HAVE JOURNEYED IN THE PAST AND RECORDED THEIR MEMORIES IN THE FORM OF PICTURES AND SYMBOLS. THE MAP REPRESENTS THE CUMULATIVE WISDOM OF GENERATIONS OF TRAVELERS, PUT TOGETHER FOR THE BENEFIT OF THOSE NOW WISHING TO MAKE THAT SAME JOURNEY. TO UNDERTAKE A JOURNEY WITH A MAP IS THEREFORE TO RELY ON THE WISDOM OF THE PAST. IT IS TO BENEFIT FROM THE HARD-WON KNOWLEDGE OF THOSE WHO HAVE EXPLORED THE UNKNOWN AND BRAVED DANGER IN ORDER TO SERVE THOSE WHO WILL FOLLOW IN THEIR FOOTSTEPS. BEHIND THE LINES AND SYMBOLS OF THE MAP LIE COUNTLESS PERSONAL STORIES—STORIES THE MAP ITSELF CAN NEVER TELL. YET SOMETIMES THOSE STORIES NEED TO BE TOLD, JUST AS THE HARD-WON INSIGHTS OF COPING WITH TRAVELING CAN ENCOURAGE, INSPIRE, AND ASSIST US.[4]

ALISTER MCGRATH

I felt like a kid again. And for a moment, I probably was.

As a boy, when my family would take trips to the lake on weekends, we played a game to see who could spot the lake first. And because we knew the precise bend in the road that gave us the first glimpse, we would each stretch up tall and then finally burst: "I SEE THE LAKE!" This was often said too soon, and always too loud. Protests followed, and laughter . . . and mom took her fingers from her ears.

And now here I sat again, a grown man with a boy's heart thumping as the tour leader announced, "Jerusalem is just over this next hill."

The next hill!

The long, slow grind up through the hills of the Judean Wilderness stretches about 18 miles from Jericho to the summit of the Mount of Olives. Not far from the modern highway on which I traveled lies the Ascent of Adummim where Jesus made His way up from Jericho to Jerusalem just before His death. (I'd love to hike up this road one day!) On this road, the Good Samaritan of Jesus' parable helped a traveler in distress. In this same wilderness, John the Baptist preached. Here, David watched over his father's flocks. I could see, in fact, the ancient tracks on the hills where shepherds still lead their flocks and of which David wrote, "He guides me in the paths of righteousness" (Ps. 23:3). This winding way snakes up nearly 4,000 feet in elevation toward the watershed of the Hill Country of Israel. And I had almost come to the top. Almost to Jerusalem.

Craning my neck as high as I could, I waited to capture that first view of the city I had imagined all my life. Suddenly, we reached the crest. And there it was below me . . . a panoramic view crowned with the golden Dome of the Rock. I saw Jerusalem. I really, really saw it.

But no shafts of light from heaven. No angels singing the "Hallelujah Chorus." Not even a respectful hush on the bus of travelers with me. Just a few clicks from cameras and horns from the cars behind. I saw the city of Jerusalem . . . in all its ordinariness.

And it remains one of the most special moments of my life.

Because there before me stood, in undeniable authenticity, the place I'd only seen in pictures and in my mind's eye. And while I'm no mystic, there was something so emotional, so experiential, *so real*—almost overwhelming—about looking down at the word "Jerusalem" in my Bible and then looking up to see the place itself.

For me, taking a trip to the Holy Land wasn't like taking a trip to the Bahamas. It wasn't a vacation as much as an education . . . and an inspiration. Some parts of Israel's culture—as with any foreign country—seemed, well, so *foreign* to me. But the oddities I observed often found their roots in places familiar, such as the Old Testament. In that way, taking a trip to Israel felt like taking a trip inside the Bible. It wasn't just seeing the sites that gave me insight into the Scriptures. The whole experience took me there.

Take the Sabbath, for instance. I remember growing up in America with "blue laws" that legislated the closing of stores on Sundays—now a thing of the past. But for many Jews in Israel, observing the Sabbath remains a religious duty. For others, it's just a good reason to take off work. From sundown Friday to sundown Saturday, Jewish businesses close, one sees fewer cars on the street, and life generally slows down.

Even elevators slow down. The hotels have special "Sabbath elevators" that stop on every floor on the Sabbath so that you don't have to "work" to push buttons. How long do you think that would last in Chicago on a Saturday? Riding up the elevator to my floor made me wonder (since I had so much time) if carrying my luggage and using my room key defeated the purpose of the Sabbath elevator. I also wondered, more seriously, how much of my true piety comes only because my culture accommodates it? Do I obey God with my elevators but compromise with my room keys? How much of my culture—even my Christian culture—gives me the false sense of godliness when really I'm just blindly following tradition? Go to church, sing the songs, give the money . . . and I'm spiritual. It's not an easy, or even comfortable, question to answer.

Most hotels in the Holy Land also supply kosher meals (and great coffee). No matter how many times I go to Israel, I always discover something about the Bible I never expected to learn. Going through a buffet line gave me insight into, of all things, the book of Leviticus. Once we stayed in a hotel by the Sea of Galilee during *Shavuot*, the Feast of the Weeks (we know it as Pentecost), the Jewish holiday celebrating the harvest season. I saw many ultra-orthodox Jews vacationing in the hotel, eating and enjoying the holiday. At mealtimes, the hotel reserved a special place for us Gentiles to eat. But we got our food from the same buffet as everyone else. Among my selections, I chose some roast and also some yogurt. Bad idea. An ultra-orthodox gentleman suddenly appeared beside me, pointed back and forth between the roast and the yogurt, and muttered in broken English that I couldn't eat those items together. He was referring to Exodus 34:26 that says not to boil a goat in its mother's milk, which has been misunderstood to mean people shouldn't eat meat and milk during the same meal. Even if it were true, it's not a *timeless* truth, for Abraham had no qualms in serving both—even to God (see Gen. 18:8)!

Now, although the Bible doesn't really teach that, their culture *does* teach it. So, because this man knew I was a Christian, I politely put back the yogurt with my apologies, lest I offend him. Afterwards, I couldn't help think of Timothy, whom Paul circumcised so as to not offend the Jews to whom they witnessed (see Acts 16:1-3). I figured I had it easy just putting back my yogurt.

On another occasion, I saw some tasty-looking meat being served by a hotel staff member. I couldn't tell what the meat was, so I pointed to it and asked the Jewish man, "Is this ham?" He just looked at me. (Yes, I really asked that. I felt pretty idiotic.)

The rule about not mixing meat and milk has serious implications for fast food: no cheeseburgers at kosher McDonald's. I remember seeing fish on the menu at one McDonald's in Beersheba. The Hebrew word for "fish" is *dag*, pronounced "dog." How does a "Mac Dog" sound for lunch? It's a good thing the menu was in Hebrew, or the place would have cleared!

Before I went to the Holy Land, the kosher laws of Leviticus seemed just words on a page. Although all of the biblical standards for dietary laws aren't represented in modern Israel (I've since learned that the hotel made a mistake in serving both milk and meat during the same meal), the fact that any *are* observed serves as a powerful illustration of what God first intended the diet code to accomplish. Even in the Garden of Eden, with the first dietary law given to eat from any tree but one (see Gen. 2:16-17), God's command centered around one question: Would they obey?

But food also had another purpose: to teach God's people to make a distinction between what is clean and unclean—or holy and unholy. When we read Leviticus 11, we notice the repeated words "unclean to you." These dietary commands represented a microcosm of the life of a Hebrew. Unclean animals represented pagan nations; clean animals represented the Hebrew nation; the sacrificial animals represented the priests.[5] Food illustrated and facilitated this separation.

God used acquired taste to assist godly living. For example, if I don't like Italian food, I probably won't go to an Italian restaurant, *and thus Italian culture won't influence me.* This is the whole point. Food served as a means to keep God's people protected from godless influences. But ironically, just as the kosher laws kept God's people apart from the nations, so Jesus' statement that all foods are now clean represented taking the good news *to the nations* (see Acts 10:9-15,34-35).

Even though Jesus put bacon back on the menu, eating still remains an important indicator of holiness—even for Christians. When we eat the Lord's Supper as a memorial to Christ, it implies our fellowship with God and other believers (see 1 Cor. 11:17-34). Believers are told to be self-controlled, a part of holiness that extends also to eating (see Titus 1:8,12-13). The Scriptures tell believers not to eat with those under church discipline (see 1 Cor. 5:11). Paul summarized it well when he wrote, "Whether, then, you eat or drink or whatever you do, do all to the glory of God" (1 Cor. 10:31).

Seeing the kosher laws applied—even misapplied—while staying in Israel reminded me that a kosher walk with God isn't about food per se. It never was. God cares less about rules than He does about holiness. (Sometimes it takes us decades to learn the difference.) Holiness means we live like Christ, distinct from the way the world lives—not because we're better, but because we worship a better God.

I guess I could experience these cultural idiosyncrasies, even biblical ones, at many places in the world. But I couldn't experience the land of the Bible anywhere else. And this remains the most valuable—even life-changing—part of my time there.

Seeing the city of Jerusalem for the first time that day immediately connected me with Scripture. After topping the Mount of Olives, we paused on the campus of Hebrew University that overlooks the city from atop Mount Scopus, or ancient Nob. Here David retrieved Goliath's sword from Ahimelech the priest when fleeing from Saul (see 1 Sam. 22). Here Sennacherib halted and shook his fist at Jerusalem at the end of his murderous rampage south through Israel and Judah, being unable to defeat Hezekiah because of God's protection (see Isa. 10:32; 37:33-37).

From a distance, only the huge, darkened walls that surrounded the Old City suggested its antiquity. Jerusalem's walls have expanded and contracted over the centuries like the breathing of a living being. The present ramparts remain best described, in my opinion, by the title of the Ottoman sultan Suliman who built them well over four centuries ago: Magnificent.

I walked atop these walls one day, a unique and wonderful way to see both inside and outside the Old City. Ascending the wall at the Jaffa Gate on the western side of the city, I peered over into the grounds of the Citadel. Built by Herod the Great, the palace also served as Pontius Pilate's quarters, and probably also the Praetorium where he condemned Jesus (see John 19:9-16). I headed counterclockwise on top of the wall and then east toward the Zion Gate. To the right sat the site on modern Mount Zion where Jesus had the Last Supper with His disciples in an upper room. Further south, I saw the infamous Hinnom Valley, which today hosts concerts and offers lush, green grass for families with Frisbees. But in the days of Judah's kings, the gorge accommodated horrific acts of idol worship and child sacrifice.

To the left (or inside the walls) lay the Armenian Quarter, a section of the city more easily seen from the ramparts than from the ground. High walls and few windows surround this sector of Jerusalem. I have to smile at the name of one of the small churches there: St. James the Cut-Up, which refers to the manner of St. James of Persia's martyrdom, not to his sense of humor. Passing the Zion Gate, still riddled with bullet holes from the 1948 War of Independence, I descended the ramparts at the Dung Gate in the Jewish Quarter, my favorite part of the Old City.

The Western Wall dominates the Jewish Quarter as the most sacred place in all Judaism. For Jews, this place is as close as they can get to worshiping on the Temple Mount. I first saw the wall at night— a breathtaking sight. These huge, towering stones formed the western side of the retaining wall that supported Herod the Great's enlargement of the Temple Mount in 20 B.C. Each stone, chiseled with Herod's signature relief around its edges, sits perfectly placed without mortar. Jesus would have seen these stones many, many times.

Men and women are separated, but anyone can pray at the wall, provided the men cover their heads. I forgot my hat once, so I was issued a small cardboard *yarmulke* that looked a lot like a french fry tray. As I approached the wall, I noticed where people had scratched out prayers on bits of paper and stuffed them into the cracks of the wall, almost as if the wall had become the priest.

I enjoyed just watching those who prayed at the wall. As I observed their rocking back and forth, I wondered, *Do they really long to know God? Do they long to honor Him? Is He their consuming passion, or is He just their national mascot?* I wondered if they, like the Jews in Jesus' day, would choose national security over a true connection to the Father.

I confess I questioned the genuineness of one young ultra-orthodox man who rocked back and forth with his prayer book but incessantly looked around to see what was going on and who was showing up. An elderly Jewish woman impressed me much more. Dressed in drab, plain clothes, she prayed at a distance with her face in her hands . . . and for quite some time. I know her prayers were private, but I would have loved to have heard the translation.

Rocking back and forth during prayer seems strange to Christians, whose worship is often private (even in public) and usually reserved. We think we're spiritual when we pray over meals at restaurants, but many Jews come to the wall several times each day to pray, read, study and socialize. And that's not all.

I discovered some come to witness, too. One Jewish woman approached me at the wall one evening. She somehow knew my affiliation with a radio ministry and told me we needed to broadcast God's way to be saved to the nations. I told her that was, in fact, our passion. She smiled and shook her head, and then shared with me a list of what all Gentiles need to do to be saved. I recognized some of the standards as being from the Ten Commandments, and I told her so. Again, she smiled and shook her head.

"*Those* commandments are for the Jews," she said.

"Do you keep them?" I asked.

"Yes."

"Perfectly?"

"No, but when I don't, I pray and promise not to break them again."

"And when you break them again, what do you do?"

"On Yom Kippur, all sins are forgiven." (She was referring to the Day of Atonement in Leviticus 16, when God annually forgave Israel's sins through the death of a sacrificial substitute.)

"But Yom Kippur required the death of a sacrifice on your behalf," I replied. "What do you do about that?"

"We have no Temple where we can sacrifice, so we just pray."

"That's not enough," I said kindly. "God is holy, and Yom Kippur required a sacrifice for your sins, not just prayers."

"When the Messiah comes," she told me, "he will explain all things and make them right." I thought of Jesus' compassion for the woman at the well who had said almost the same words to Him (see John 4:25). So I told this daughter of Abraham standing before me that I believed her Messiah *had* already come, that His name was *Yeshua*, and that He paid the final sacrifice for her sins with His own life just a few hundred yards behind her. And He would come once more to Israel.

That didn't go over well. She shook her head again, but now she wasn't smiling.

We lobbed the volleyball back and forth a few more times before she began to back away, talking so that I couldn't interrupt her and again telling me to announce a salvation by works.

As she turned to leave, I felt a great sadness. As Paul wrote, "For I testify about them that they have a zeal for God, but not in accordance with knowledge. For not knowing about God's righteousness and seeking to establish their own, they did not subject themselves to the righteousness of God. For Christ is the end of the law for righteousness to everyone who believes" (Rom. 10:2-4). I don't remember this woman's name, but God does. Please pray for her and for those like her; she represents what nearly all Jewish people believe today.

The Western Wall stretches much further north than the stones the newsreels show. The majority of the wall lies buried and remains accessible only through a narrow tunnel underground. I've walked a number of times through the passageway that follows the wall its full length. It boggles my mind how the builders moved these stones around. One in particular is massive—the largest of its kind in the Middle East. The reason this part of the wall remains buried and unexcavated stems from the fact that it lays underneath a part of the city whose residents remain completely unsympathetic to Jewish history—the Muslim Quarter.

The Muslim Quarter covers the lion's share of the Old City, including the Temple Mount. The Western Wall tunnel emerges beside the Umariyya Boys' School, where the Antonia Fortress sat in Paul's day. As I stood there and gazed out the windows at the Temple Mount compound below, I envisioned myself as Paul who, after his arrest, addressed a crowd below from a similar vantage on the stairs of the Antonia (see Acts 21:35–22:34). What courage and compassion he must have had.

Five times each day, the entire city must endure loudspeakers (emphasis on *loud*) featuring Muslim prayers and chanting. Yet I love the irony that within the Muslim Quarter itself sits the most beautiful church in Jerusalem, a Crusader cathedral named after St. Anne. Its stone walls offer such superior acoustics that most Christians who visit can't resist offering songs of praise that rise to honor the Lord Jesus. What poetic irony.

The Christian Quarter has as its sole claim to fame the Church of the Holy Sepulcher. As I shared in the devotional for Day 44, the church offers plenty to offend evangelical sensibilities. Traditionalism stifles the place. In fact, if the historical tradition wasn't so strong that Jesus died and rose at this site, one would walk away in disgust. Many do anyway.

But somehow, I was able to look past the religious veneer and to focus on the event it has attempted to conceal. I entered the church, went straight up the stairs to the right, and leaned against the cold walls that faced ancient Golgotha. There, behind a façade of incense burners, crucifixes, icons and a parade of worshipers who kiss the rock beneath the altar, lies the spot where God redeemed the entire universe. It's unseen, indistinct and unrecognizable, but present nonetheless.

Almost every day, I relive the experience I had in the church, as do most believers in Christ. We always have to look past the façade to the real reason our lives have meaning, don't we? Jesus died for our sins and rose again. It's a historical fact. No amount of religious trinkets or traditionalism can cover that glorious truth. Each time I go to the Church of the Holy Sepulcher, I like to remember this. That way, it's never a wasted trip.

One of the cultural (and often comical) rules required at many holy sites in Israel involves wearing modest dress. "Modesty" is defined as having everyone's heads and shoulders covered. Men are required to wear long pants and women to wear pants or skirts covering their knees. I still remember the tour leader on our first trip to Israel saying, "You can be immodest here." But in places where the rule exists, they're quite serious about it. I've seen women, who from most standards seemed perfectly modest, scolded and asked to leave a site because they failed to cover their shoulders.

I once entered the Dominus Flevit church on the Mount of Olives and began photographing the city of Jerusalem through the church's unique window. After some time, I noticed that my friend James was nowhere around. He suddenly appeared, but in a manner in which I never hope to see him again. Because he hadn't worn modest dress that day, the gatekeeper loaned him a wrap-around skirt to wear to cover his knees! That redefined my definition of modesty, I believe, a bit too much! He has yet to live it down.

* * * *

As wonderful as the Holy City is to see, Israel offers much more to experience than Jerusalem.

At Caesarea by the Sea, I smelled the same salty air as Peter did when he first preached there to the Gentiles (see Acts 10). And I felt the cool Mediterranean breezes that would have refreshed Paul as he emerged from his prison to make his defense before Agrippa (see Acts 25).

From Mount Carmel, where Elijah had his showdown with the prophets of Baal, I've seen the Jezreel Valley's broad expanse and stood dumbfounded at the armies of world history that have trudged across this plain and fought historical battles that predated even Israel.

On the far side of the valley, I stood on a ridge that encircles Nazareth like the rim of a bowl. Jesus, like any boy growing up in Nazareth, would have known the ins and outs of the hills that surrounded His village. Certainly, He would have seen the valley from this ridge many times. Glancing to the left, He could see Mount Tabor rising above the valley floor and could imagine the armies of Deborah and Barak as they raced down into the valley to face Sisera. Further beyond, He could see the area where Gideon camped to face the Midianites. Glancing even further to Mount Gilboa, Jesus could remember the tragic life of Saul that ended on its slopes. All this He could see from the ridge of His boyhood hometown. But another battle lay across the valley, a battle future still. Through the distant haze and far into the future, Jesus could squint and see the hill of Megiddo to the southwest, the site of Armageddon in the book of Revelation.

As I stood there, I imagined He would have thought about the history that stretched out before Him. How could He not have?

On the northern shore of the Sea of Galilee, I've stood on the hill where crowds would have stood to hear Jesus' Parable of the Sower (see Day 19). Amazingly, with a friend reading the parable from the cove by the lake—approximately where Jesus would have preached from a boat—I could hear his voice clearly from where I stood on the hill. Jesus chose a place where thousands could hear His message, without Him having to scream.

In America, we put our 200-year-old artifacts behind glass and lasers in the Smithsonian Institute. But in Israel, I've walked up and touched stones Jesus could have touched. While there are many sites today where one can still reasonably assert that "Jesus was here," most references to "here" have to be general to be honest. But Jacob's well near modern-day Nablus is a place where Christ truly stood. When my wife and I paused beside the well and drew water from its deep source, we read the words Jesus spoke in that very spot so long ago. The words didn't seem more true to me having read them at this place, but the impact of Jesus' words sank deeper in my heart because the visual He used was right before me and dripped from my hands: "Everyone who drinks of this water shall thirst again; but whoever drinks of the water that I shall give him shall never thirst; but the water that I shall give him shall become in him a well of water springing up to eternal life" (John 4:13-14).

It's impossible to appreciate the wilderness wanderings of Israel until you've stumbled around in the places where the Israelites grumbled against God (see Num. 20:1-2). Most everywhere in these inhospitable places, no life exists at all. Once while traveling through the Desert of Zin in southern Israel, we read from Deuteronomy 8:1-3, where Moses reminded Israel why God led them through the wilderness: "that He might humble you, testing you, to know what was in your heart, whether you would keep His commandments or not" (v. 2).

Our bus stopped in the desert for half an hour, and each of us headed in a different direction to spend some time with God. I took some water and a small Bible and found a secluded spot in the sun among the stones and lizards. The crunching beneath my feet revealed layers of dark, sharp flint, which stretched from horizon to horizon and reflected the sun like a mirror. Sitting down in this lonely place, I imagined the Hebrews' mournful journey as they sojourned 40 long years on account of their disbelief and disobedience to God. What a lesson in wasted time.

I began to reflect on my own wilderness wanderings and prayed for God to help me to bring specific parts of my life under submission to Him. I remembered that Israel's first act after they crossed the Jordan River into the Promised Land was to set up stones to memorialize the event (see Josh. 4:5-7). Before I made my way back to the bus, I found two large stones and set them on edge as memorials to my prayer.

After one such excursion in this wilderness, one of our traveling companions, a Houston pastor named Henry, boarded the motor coach with a sweat-soaked shirt, and collapsed in his seat. When asked if he could now understand why the Israelites grumbled against God, he answered, "I'm with them!" and extracted a long swallow from his canteen.

God has answered my wilderness prayer. But it didn't come about because I traveled to Israel, prayed a prayer, and set up two stones in the Wilderness of Zin. As I look back over the years since that half-hour I spent in the desert, I can see His hand guiding me through days I would never have chosen—days of deep distress, loneliness, financial crises, heartrending deaths and bitter disillusionment with people and with my own dreams. I've come to recognize that God changed me in the same way, remarkably, that He changed the Hebrews. He taught me to surrender as He took me to painful places. And He loved me enough to take me there.

*　*　*　*

Many places in the land of the Bible have familiar names: the Sea of Galilee, Jerusalem, Jericho and the Mount of Olives. Yet without an understanding of where each name fits in relation to another, the places can seem disheveled in our minds—like spilled puzzle pieces without the top of the box for perspective.

I shared this frustration. For the vast majority of my Christian life and ministry, the benefits of understanding the land of the Bible remained hidden like artifacts in the sand. I possessed knowledge of the place names, but they played no role in my study of the Bible except to distract and confuse me. Because I couldn't appreciate a site's contribution to the biblical narrative, I dismissed the unfamiliar as irrelevant or, at the very least, of minor importance.

But when my wife and I took our first trip to Israel . . . it all changed.

I rank the experience of learning biblical geography on the level of learning Hebrew and Greek—probably even higher. I discovered an integral part of Bible study I had missed all my life. Like seeing the whole puzzle put together, I was now able to see the individual sites in light of the whole. I became aware of a cohesion and logic as to why God included geography in the inspired text. My memory of biblical events was strengthened by associating the events with their geographical locations. What I had dismissed earlier as irrelevant I began to recognize as an essential part of God's dealing with His people.

Today, we live in an age in which traveling great distances and finding something to drink no longer prove a challenge. Our transportation system requires little more than a basic understanding of road signs and airline gates (which somehow I still seem to miss!). Consequently, we feel very little need to know any geography. And we take that ignorance into our study of the Bible. I know I did.

Before we come to Scripture and ask, "What does this passage mean to me?" we must understand what it means in context, including what it meant to the original readers. Context is not just the words before and after the passage but also includes history and geography, and thus reveals their value in our study and application of the Scriptures. It may seem an overstatement to claim that a person must study biblical geography to understand the Bible, but it's fair to say that the study will take a person much further toward an accurate understanding of God's Word.

A recent survey administered during the course of doctoral research revealed some astounding statistics. For 97 percent of those who took the survey, taking a class on biblical geography improved their understanding of the Bible. In addition, 98 percent of people reported that traveling to Israel provided them far more than what books ever could. And an astounding 99 percent of those who have traveled to Israel agreed that experiencing the Holy Land had strengthened their spiritual life.[6]

Don't misunderstand these results. Studying biblical geography won't provide some long-lost secret to a higher spiritual life. And traveling to Israel won't gain you more favor with God. But the journey provides a deeper, clearer and more vibrant understanding of the truth that God has already revealed. That truth—God's Word—changes lives.

Going to Israel, in my own experience, permanently marked my life and changed the way I understand the Bible. Places and names that I used to pass over now immediately bring to mind a site's history, its military benefits, its scenery and even its smells. Having knowledge of a passage's geography gives me a head start as I attempt to understand why events took place—sometimes repeatedly—in certain locations.

In Israel, I quickly realized that God keeps quiet about the significance of most places. No holograph angel appeared beside the road and discussed each place's significance. The Bible bursts with geographical references, but they never yielded their fruit to me as a casual observer. But for those who peer into the text for its details and open an atlas . . . my, what treasures await! Jesus said, "If I speak of earthly things and you do not believe, how will you believe if I speak of heavenly things?" The truth we see in earthly, physical things gives credence to those heavenly untouchables God tells us about.

What is it that causes millions to come to Israel each year? To kiss the rocks, tour the shrines and genuflect along each station of the Via Dolorosa? I don't know. I can only tell you what going to the Holy Land did for me. Walking the land of Israel has provided me with a deeper appreciation of God as the Lord of world history and also seemingly minor details—both of which bring extreme comfort to my life. I learned that my relationship with Christ involves my whole person and that God desires to employ all the senses He created in me to enhance my relationship with Him. I discovered that when I study the Bible, having seen where its events actually occurred, the Holy Spirit uses more than words to teach me. More than knowledge, the relationship involves my emotion and imagination. Far from mysticism, these very subjective elements can be used in studying the objective truth of God's Word.

I felt like a kid again when I first saw Jerusalem. Probably because coming to the Holy Land gave my faith a newness and a youthfulness—a first love, of sorts—because I better understood what God was saying in His Word.

God used these places to mold the lives of His people in the biblical narrative. And if you will allow Him, He can use it to change your life as well. Begin to recognize that all the places God takes you—many of them painful—have nothing but His glory and your best interests in mind.

The irony of going places with God is that the One who travels with us is also our destination. He takes us to these places to give us more of Himself.

I find it fascinating that even our journey to heaven will lead us again to earth. If we interpret our Old and New Testaments literally— if God really meant what He said to Israel and to the Church—then the Messiah will one day reign on earth from Jerusalem over a literal kingdom. And we who love Him will reign with Him.

I enjoy knowing that I can always look forward to going to Israel again . . . at least one more time.

ENDNOTES

1. See *New International Version* study notes on Genesis 49:4 for further explanation.

2. Nogah Hareuveni, *Nature in Our Biblical Heritage*, trans. Helen Frenkley (Kiryat Ono, Israel: Neot Kedumim, 1980), pp. 49-52.

3. Jerome Murphy-O'Connor, *The Holy Land: An Oxford Archaeological Guide: From Earliest Times to 1700*, fourth ed. (New York: Oxford University Press, 1998), p. 45.

4. Alister E. McGrath, *The Journey: A Pilgrim in the Lands of the Spirit*, 1st ed. (New York: Doubleday, 2000), pp. 21-22.

5. Allen P. Ross, *Holiness to the Lord: A Guide to the Exposition of the Book of Leviticus* (Grand Rapids, MI: Baker Academic, 2002), pp. 250-265.

6. D. Wayne Stiles II, *The Benefits of Understanding and Experiencing the Historical Geography of Israel* (D.Min. Dissertation, Dallas Theological Seminary, 2004), p. 76.

SCRIPTURE INDEX

SITE/SUBJECT INDEX

Dear Friend,

Before you ever picked up this book, I prayed for you.

I prayed that the seeds it would plant in your heart would help you along the journey that God has for you as He takes you to the places of His choosing.

Feel free to visit my website for helpful links on including biblical geography and suggested resources in your study of God's Word. The site also contains articles, recommended links and a variety of content to encourage your spiritual journey . . . at whatever stage you find yourself along the way.

For speaking engagements, questions or generally edifying comments, feel free to contact me via the website. I may not be able to respond to all mail personally, but I enjoy hearing from you.

I appreciate your prayers, and I continue to pray for you as well.

Thank you for taking this journey with me,

Wayne Stiles

www.waynestiles.com

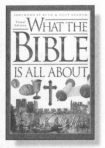

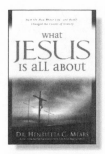

Now You Can Walk Where Jesus Walked!

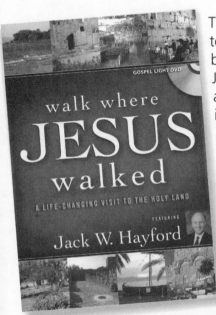

The Bible comes to life in this video tour, which is the next best thing to being there! Discover the life of Jesus as He was revealed in the Old and New Testaments, as well as His impact on the Holy Land today and in the future. Venture to the Holy Land, overlooking the ancient city of Jerusalem from atop the Mount of Olives. Gaze across the Kidron valley while listening to the inspiring teaching of one of America's leading pastors, Jack Hayford. Then travel on to key biblical sites, such as:

Jericho • The Garden Tomb
Bethlehem • Galilee
Megiddo • Caesarea and more.

Walk Where Jesus Walked DVD • 70 minutes • UPC 607135009320

Available at Bookstores Everywhere!

Visit **www.regalbooks.com** to join **Regal's FREE e-newsletter**. You'll get useful **excerpts from our newest releases** and **special access to online chats with your favorite authors**. Sign up today!

Regal
God's Word for Your World
www.regalbooks.com